# Mastering
# ACCOUNTING
# RESEARCH
## for the CPA Exam

**2nd**
EDITION

# Mastering
# ACCOUNTING
# RESEARCH
## *the* CPA Exam

2nd EDITION

### Anita L. Feller

WILEY

JOHN WILEY & SONS, INC.

For general information on our other products and services, or technical support, please contact our Customer Care Department within the United States at 800-762-2974, outside the United States at 317-572-3993 or fax 317-572-4002.

Wiley also publishes its books in a variety of electronic formats. Some content that appears in print may not be available in electronic books.
For more information about Wiley products, visit our Web site at http://www.wiley.com.

*Library of Congress Cataloging-in-Publication Data*

Feller, Anita L.
    Mastering accounting research for the CPA exam / Anita L. Feller. – 2nd ed.
      p. cm.
    Includes index.
    ISBN 978-0-470-29338-6 (pbk.)
    1. Accounting – Research. 2. Financial accounting research system. 3. Accounting – United States – Examinations – Study guides. I. Title.
    HF5661.F37 2008
    657—dc22

                                        2008004970

Printed in the United States of America
10  9  8  7  6  5  4  3  2  1

*For our future*
*Certified Public Accountants*

# CONTENTS

# ABOUT THE AUTHOR

Anita Feller holds a B.S. in Finance, a M.S. Accountancy in Taxation, and a Ph.D. in Education from the University of Illinois. Throughout her career at the University of Illinois, she has taught a variety of courses. Her areas of teaching include introductory accounting, taxation, advanced accounting, institutions and regulations, and applied professional research. She is an Editor for the *Wiley CPA Exam Review in Financial Accounting and Reporting*, and a coauthor of *Applied Professional Research for Accountants* with David A. Ziebart. She also teaches CPA Review courses in the FAR and BEC areas. Most of all, she loves teaching applied professional accounting research.

# ACKNOWLEDGMENTS

I would like to thank the AICPA for their efforts on the new computer-based CPA exam and for providing such a valuable Web site to help candidates prepare for the exam. A special acknowledgment goes to the programmers of Folio Views for creating the most user-friendly, powerful tool in accounting research. Another special thank you goes to Cornell University Law Library for creating the most user-friendly, organized, and attractive Web site for the tax code.

Personal thanks should be given to several colleagues. I would like to thank Professor Larry Tomassini for his encouragement to join the academic community. I would like to thank Professor Dave Ziebart for his pioneering efforts in teaching applied professional research at the University of Illinois. I would also like to thank Debra Hopkins, Director of the CPA Review Program at Northern Illinois University. Her dedication, teaching excellence, and expertise have always been an inspiration to me.

Finally, I would like to thank John DeRemigis, Judy Howarth, Natasha Andrews-Noel, and Pam Reh at John Wiley & Sons, Inc. who believed in this project and made this book possible.

# INTRODUCTION

## What This Book Can Do For You

Congratulations on your decision to sit for the CPA exam! Yes, like those who went before you, you *can* pass the exam.

You've survived all those technical accounting courses, advanced courses, systems, auditing, cost, and tax, and now you're ready to take the big exam. But perhaps in those intermediate or advanced courses, you didn't receive enough exposure to research in the accounting standards, the auditing standards, or the tax code.

No problem! This little book is designed to quickly bring you up to speed on the research component. We (you and this little book) will explore Financial Accounting Research System (FARS), the AICPA professional standards, and the Internal Revenue Code.

The goal is that you have a good overview of the organization of the authoritative literature, knowledge of the standards, and strategies for researching the infobases for FAR, AUD, and REG. Our ultimate goal is to bring you up to speed quickly.

# 1 RESEARCH AND THE CPA EXAM

## THE COMPUTER-BASED CPA EXAM

The computer-based CPA exam is here to stay. Over 100,000 candidates have taken the exam since its inception in April, 2004[1]. The computer-based CPA Exam can test a candidate's work-related skills by using small cases called simulations. These simulations are minicases that require multiple tasks including communications and research.

The simulations component has replaced the old problems, other objective format questions, and essays on the old paper-pencil exam. Not to worry! In many ways, the newer simulations component is actually easier for the CPA candidate because candidates are no longer required to structure the problem. Candidates no longer create the schedules, tables, and disclosures. Instead, the answer formats are created, and the candidate fills in the blanks.

Since the simulations are machine-graded, the simulation is broken into parts. Some parts may require matching exercises, completing a table, or calculating values. Other parts may require selecting an answer from a list of choices on a drop-down menu. Simulation questions with drop-down menus are similar to multiple-choice questions. Near the end of each simulation is a communications component, which is similar to the essay component in the old paper-pencil exam. Again, the computerized exam is easier, because candidates can easily edit the essay and use a spell-checker.

The newest part of the CPA exam is the research component which is included in each of the simulations. In the paper-pencil exam, it was good enough to know the rules. Now the candidate must know the rules *and* find them!

## RESEARCH COMPONENTS ON THE EXAM

There are three different research components on the computer-based CPA exam. Research is tested separately in the Financial Accounting and Reporting (FAR), Auditing and Attestation (AUD), and Regulation (REG) portions of the CPA exam. Therefore, candidates must be knowledgeable and skilled with each of these infobases.

In each of the three areas (FAR, AUD, and REG), the research requirements and the infobases are completely different. The infobases contain information from several sources: the Financial Accounting Standards Board, the Public Company Accounting Oversight Board, the American Institute of Certified Public Accountants, and the US Treasury Department.

---

[1] *Source:* **The Uniform CPA Examination Alert,** *Fall 2007, AICPA Web site.*

Because these products contain different information, it is important that you are familiar with each resource and infobase, as well as the CPA exam interface.

The Financial Accounting and Reporting (FAR) simulations require research in the financial accounting literature that is found in the Financial Accounting Research System, called FARS. The FARS infobase is a collection of accounting pronouncements and is copyrighted by the Financial Accounting Standards Board (FASB). Both the Original Pronouncements as Amended and the Current Text are available on the exam. In the FAR simulations, a candidate may be required to cite one paragraph or citation from the financial accounting standards to answer a question or research problem in each simulation.

In the AUD simulations, the infobases tested are the AICPA Professional Standards and/or the PCAOB Standards. Candidates may be required to complete one or two tasks within a given simulation. An audit simulation may include a research task to solve a case by finding a rule or rules from the auditing standards. An audit simulation may also require the candidate to copy up to ten paragraphs from the auditing standards for a reporting requirement.

In the REG simulations, research skills are tested in the tax area. The literature accessed in the REG simulations may include the Internal Revenue Tax Code and/or Publication 17 published by the US Department of Treasury. For REG, candidates will be required to find the applicable code section. Publication 17 may be required to complete a tax return.

## STUDYING RESEARCH FOR THE CPA EXAM

It is important to outline a reasonable set of goals in preparing for the research component on the CPA exam. A candidate should develop a quick study strategy for attaining these goals. First, a candidate must become familiar with the commercial infobases or the hard copy of the professional literature. Second, it is essential to link this knowledge to already existing technical knowledge. Finally, every candidate must learn to use the interface of the CPA exam. Knowing the interface and search commands will save valuable time on the CPA exam.

As you study, think strategically about which questions are most likely to be asked. The current CPA exam does not require that you solve a challenging or complex case; the exam requires that you solve a minicase by locating a specific definition or rule in the literature. Keep in mind: The exam will not ask for a candidate's opinion; it will ask a research question that has one correct answer.

Many candidates believe they can rely on keyword searches during the exam. The problem with keyword searches is that they produce too many results to sort through and read during the exam's limited time. Therefore, success on the research component is more likely if one is familiar with certain standards, and the researcher knows approximately where to look for the answer. This text will explore the overview and organization of the authoritative literature for FAR, AUD, and REG so that candidates have a good understanding of where certain information is located in the literature.

For the financial accounting standards, the text will take an historical perspective to look at the pronouncements. It is easier to find information if you have an overview of when certain standards were issued, and when certain topics were hot issues in the business environment. This book will also look at the structure of the different accounting pronouncements. Knowing the structure of the standard is important for moving through the pronouncement quickly.

Finally, this text will give special attention to vocabulary. Candidates can capitalize on knowing certain accounting jargon that may help find the answer quickly. Practicing research skills will also help strengthen a candidate's knowledge of the various accounting topics. Therefore, studying research is great for preparing for the exam!

## OBTAINING THE AUTHORITATIVE LITERATURE

### Financial Accounting and Reporting Literature

The financial accounting and reporting literature is the property of the Financial Accounting Standards Board (FASB). The FASB posts the Statements of Financial Accounting Standards online at www.fasb.org. Although these pronouncements can be downloaded in .pdf format, the original pronouncements have not been updated to show amended or superseded materials. In addition, the FASB Statements are not formatted in a way that allows keyword searches. Although the FASB Web site's .pdf files are helpful in learning a new pronouncement, the site is not the optimal location for studying amended or updated material for the CPA exam.

The updated version of the FASB's literature is published by John Wiley & Sons, Inc. The Original Pronouncements as Amended and the Current Text are available in hard copy format and can be ordered from any bookstore. In addition, two electronic versions of the standards are available. These electronic versions are referred to as infobases because they are a database of information.

One version of the electronic infobase is a CD-ROM product titled *Financial Accounting Research System* (FARS). The FARS CD product uses a Folio search engine. Although the search program is loaded on the computer's hard drive, the FARS CD must remain in the CD drive to access the infobase. The FARS CD is available as a stand-alone product directly through John Wiley & Sons, Inc. at www.wiley.com. To find the CD-ROM product on the Wiley Web site, type in capital letters FARS CD and look for the 2007 edition. The CD can also be ordered from www.amazon.com.

Generally, the new version of the CD is available in August, and it costs approximately $35 before taxes, shipping, or handling charges. The 2007 edition is current through June 1, 2007, and contains all the FASB pronouncements through FAS 159.

The other electronic version of the financial accounting literature is an infobase called FARS Online. FARS Online is available for use with a one-year subscription from John Wiley & Sons, Inc. FARS Online subscriptions are listed with Wiley's Higher Education Division. Go to the Web page www.wiley.com/college/farsonline and follow the instructions to subscribe. FARS Online can also be found at http://he-cda.wiley.com. As of November 1, 2007, the subscription rate for FARS Online is $29.95 for 12 months.

Although FARS Online contains the same information as the FARS CD-ROM product, the FARS Online search engine, menus, and commands look slightly different. The best feature of FARS Online is that its menus and commands are similar to the interface used on the CPA exam.

## FARS BOOK, CD, OR FARS ONLINE—WHICH IS BEST?

Many people ask, "Which version of FARS is best?" The answer to that question depends on personal preference and the kind of work being done. For me, all three versions work because I love to do research.

The paperback books work well for writing class materials and casually reading the standards. It also provides a topical index in the back of the book. The book indicates superseded material by shading the text in gray. The book also identifies amended material by incorporating the new material into the appropriate standard with underlining or special notation. The paperback is excellent for reading the standard from front to back and highlighting important information.

For research purposes, the FARS CD is more efficient than the paperback version. The FARS CD provides a Folio search engine that is powerful and fast. The FARS executable program loads onto the hard drive of a computer, and the FARS CD must be in the CD drive to access the infobases. The FARS CD does not require an Internet connection. The CD-ROM product is perfect for learning the standards and doing professional research. One of the best features of the FARS CD is that the Folio search engine produces detailed results in chronological order. Having the results in chronological order is extremely helpful in learning the organization and content of the standards.

Of course, the FARS Online version contains the same information as the CD product, but there are three major differences. First, as its name implies, the user must be online to use FARS Online. Second, the search engine is different from the CD product. And third, the search results are presented in a different order from the results on the CD product. The FARS Online version provides results that look like Internet search results. The advanced search results are not listed in chronological order of the pronouncements. Instead, the FARS Online program prioritizes the results by an algorithm based on the relevance and frequency of key words. The results are then displayed based on the priority given by the search engine. Some researchers may find a jumbled list of results disorienting and more time-consuming to sort through. However, the important advantage to FARS Online is that its navigation and search commands are similar to the search interface on the CPA exam.

So, which version of the standards should a CPA candidate use to study for the exam? The answer to that question depends on an individual's personal budget and access to the professional infobases at his or her university or workplace. If the university or an employer has site licenses to the infobases, use those. If not, a candidate should purchase a version of FARS to learn the infobase.

Sometimes the FARS CD is adopted with a textbook in intermediate or advanced accounting classes. If you purchased a previous version of the FARS CD in an earlier accounting class, check to see if that version has expired. If not, you can use that older version to study the standards and learn the content and organization of the standards. However, if you are using an older version of the standards, be sure to get familiar with the most recent standards before the CPA exam.

If a candidate has the extra money to buy FARS Online, then buy FARS Online. Again, the CPA exam interface is similar to the FARS Online product, and it is helpful to practice with that product before the exam. Go to he-cda-wiley.com and get online with FARS!

After a candidate is familiar with the accounting standards and the infobase, it is easy to practice with the CPA sample exam interface, located on the AICPA Web site. Keep in mind, though, that the CPA sample exam has a very limited and abbreviated version of the infobase. There are not enough standards posted on the sample exam to learn the standards. The CPA sample exam is only useful to learn how to navigate on the research component.

No matter which version of the FARS infobase a candidate uses, it is important to know the organization of the financial accounting literature. In addition, it is essential that every candidate practices on the sample exam in each research area, FAR, AUD, and REG, before sitting for the CPA exam.

### Auditing and Attestation Literature

The auditing and attestation literature, AICPA Resource, is produced and copyrighted by the AICPA. Unfortunately, AICPA Resource is more costly to obtain than the FASB literature. It is available for a subscription in CD-ROM format, with quarterly updates. AICPA Resource is also available in an online subscription for AICPA members for approximately $425 per year. In addition, the AICPA Web site offers a special subscription rate to AICPA members who are CPA Candidates.

Many universities obtain a site license with quarterly updates. Also, most accounting firms subscribe to the AICPA professional literature, so many candidates have access to this infobase at their workplace. Check with your university library, computer lab, or employer to determine if the AICPA infobase is available to you without charge.

AICPA Resource can also be licensed directly from the AICPA at the AICPA Web site at www.aicpa.org. There is a special student subscription rate for student members of the AICPA. The student rate requires a candidate to join the AICPA as a student member and then subscribe to the AICPA Professional Standards for an additional fee. The membership requirements, dues, and subscription rates are posted on the AICPA Web site at www. aicpa.org.

Another source for some of the AICPA standards can be found at the Public Company Accounting Oversight Board's Web site at www.pcaob.org. There are two sets of standards at the PCAOB Web site. The PCAOB standards are labeled as Auditing Standard No. 1, Auditing Standard No. 2, up through Auditing Standard No. 5. The PCAOB standards (AS1 to AS5) relate only to the audits of publicly traded companies. However, in 2003, the PCAOB adopted the AICPA standards as its interim standards. These interim standards are to be used until superseded or amended by newer PCAOB standards. Therefore, the PCAOB has posted the interim standards for auditing, attestation, quality control, ethics, and independence.

Please note that the interim standards posted by the PCAOB are only a portion of the AICPA Professional Standards. For example, only two ethics standards are posted, ET 100 and ET 191. The AICPA Web page indicates that the Code of Professional Conduct is numbered from ET 50 through ET 500. Although the interim standards posted at the PCAOB Web site are not a complete list of the AICPA standards, and are not in keyword searchable format, enough standards are posted to help the candidate learn the structure and organization of the AICPA standards. The interim standards are posted in a drop-down menu format similar to the table of contents used in AUD research on the CPA exam.

Candidates may find that it is not necessary to purchase a copy of the AICPA Professional Standards. Why? First, you may be able to learn from the PCAOB Web site. Second, if you do not have access to the AICPA Professional Standards, you can practice on the AICPA Web site after you have received your NTS (Notice to Schedule). Every CPA candidate receives free access to this important literature for six months. Go to www.cpa-exam.org. Under the tab marked "Prepare for the Exam," click on "Access to Prof. Literature." Be sure to write down your log-in and password. Also, bookmark the Web page that has the log-in page because the log-in page can be difficult to find again unless it is bookmarked.

The auditing literature is generally easier to search than the financial accounting literature because it is codified and well organized. Hence, you may require less practice with the auditing standards. Begin your study of the audit literature as you study the auditing materials in your CPA review course. Most CPA review courses reference their study materials to the AUs, the ARs, and the ATs. Because the auditing literature uses very descriptive titles, you can usually find the answer by clicking down the menus and looking through for the correct title. You will probably need less practice in this area because everything is grouped by topic, and the titles are straightforward and intuitive.

Many candidates find that the AICPA practice site is sufficient to learn the various sections, menus, and titles of the auditing standards. Once you have studied this book and your audit CPA review materials, you should sufficiently know your way around the AICPA standards. Then you're ready to use the infobase when you receive your NTS (Notice to Schedule). Although the interface on the AICPA Web site is not exactly like the CPA exam interface, this free site provides you with excellent menus to learn the auditing standards. You can finish your studies by practicing with the real exam interface on the sample exam, also found at the AICPA Web site.

The AICPA literature is covered in depth in Chapter 6.

## Regulation Literature

Candidates may find two research resources on the Regulation portion of the CPA Exam: the Internal Revenue Code and Publication 17. You should become familiar with both of these resources before taking the Regulation part of the CPA exam.

The Internal Revenue Code (IRC) contains the laws passed by Congress. Therefore, the Code is public domain information. A Yahoo or Google search will provide several sites on the Internet for the IRC.

The Internal Revenue Service home page is www.irs.gov. If you search in the top right-hand corner for **internal revenue code,** you should find a match that shows "Tax Code, Regulations, and Official Guidance." This search usually shows a 51% match. Click on that link and find the next menu. This menu provides access to the Table of Contents of the Code, a link for Retrieve by Section number, and Execute full text search. If you read the fine print under these links, you will see that the IRC materials are provided as a public service by the Legal Information Institute of Cornell University Law School, not the IRS. Notice that you will be taken to another menu and you must click on the button "Leave IRS Site" to gain access to this infobase.

This Cornell Web site is fantastic. Cornell Law School has a beautiful, searchable code. There it is, Title 26 in all its glory—keep clicking on the table of contents menu and drill your way down into the Code just like on the CPA exam. What a beautiful site. Bookmark this for future use—this link is invaluable!

Yahoo or Google can also be used to search for other IRC sites available via the Internet. However, the Cornell is quite a beautiful site and easy to use—my personal favorite!

Another important piece of literature for the tax portion of the regulation exam is Publication 17 (Pub. 17), "Your Federal Income Tax" from the Department of the Treasury Internal Revenue Service. Currently, Pub. 17 is listed on the sample exam in REG as a resource. Therefore, it is recommended that all candidates become familiar with this document. If a simulation requires the candidate to complete a tax return, the standard deductions, personal exemptions, deduction limitations, and other information are located in Pub. 17. Knowledge of the contents and organization of Pub. 17 is important because if a candidate needs to access information in this large document, there certainly is not enough time to browse through it or read it during the exam.

To find Pub. 17, go to the IRS Web site at www.irs.gov. At the IRS main Web page, on the left-hand side, there is a link for "More Forms and Publications." Click on "More Forms and Publications." There is a menu for downloading forms. Under the section marked "Download forms and publications by:" click on "Publication Number." Then find *Publication 17 Your Federal Income Tax*. Highlight this link, and click the "Retrieve Selected Files" button. Publication 17 will download in .pdf format. It is a large document, (over 250 pages), so be patient. Downloading Pub. 17 may take some time.

If the IRS has changed its menus, then perform a search for "Publication 17." Click on Pub. 17 in the results list, and you should find appropriate instructions for downloading.

In addition to downloading Publication 17, you can obtain a complimentary copy at your local IRS office. However, if you download Pub. 17, you can practice searching it with the "find" command in Adobe .pdf. Personally, I enjoy having both the hardcopy and the downloaded version of this valuable publication.

At this time, the AICPA Web site does not have a tax infobase to practice for the REG research. There is only a small portion of the tax infobase available on the CPA sample exam. Don't worry! This text will cover the organization of the code in this book, and you can practice on the Internet. The tax literature is discussed thoroughly in Chapter 7.

## PRACTICING RESEARCH BEFORE THE EXAM

As indicated earlier, candidates can also obtain free online access to the financial accounting and auditing infobases before taking the CPA exam. The online packet includes the FASB Original Pronouncements, the FASB Current Text, and the AICPA Professional Standards. The FASB Original Pronouncements and Current Text are used in FAR; the AICPA Professional Standards are used in AUD. Candidates must have applied to take the exam and be eligible by their state board of accountancy to register for this free six-month subscription. The AICPA notes that this version of the infobases is also not identical to the version used on the CPA exam. Therefore, it is still important to read the CPA exam tutorial and practice research using the sample exam.

The AICPA will give you access to the FAR and AUD literature when you receive your Notice to Schedule. You may obtain a log-in and a password to access the infobases for FAR and AUD by visiting the AICPA Web site at www.cpa-exam.org and clicking under "Prepare for the Exam" and "Access to Prof. Literature." Make *sure* you keep the e-mail that provides the link to the log-in page, and bookmark the address. If you lose this information, you may find it difficult to locate the log-in page again. As we discussed earlier, at this time, the AICPA has not posted a practice infobase for tax.

In addition to the FAR and AUD literature, the AICPA also provides a tutorial for the CPA exam and a sample CPA exam at their Web site. Go to www.aicpa.org and click on CPA Exam. Follow the menus to exam tutorial. You can also go directly to the CPA exam Web page at www.cpa-exam.org. At the very top of the CPA Examination page, you will see "Tutorial and Sample Exams." Follow the links on that page to find the tutorial.

The CPA Exam Tutorial is great for learning the commands and interface of the exam. This tutorial is a "show and tell" version of the exam. It walks you through the various screens for entering the exam, answering multiple-choice questions, continuing on to another section of the exam, answering simulation questions, using the calculator and spreadsheet functions, using the research standards, and exiting the exam. The tutorial is very informative, but it is not interactive.

Although the tutorial is wonderful for learning the interface of the CPA exam, seeing the exam interface and using it are two different things! Just because you read the tutorial does not mean that you will know or remember all the intricate details of how the exam interface works. There is a big difference in thinking you know something, and really being able to do it. Therefore, you *must* work the sample exams. *No*—let me take that a step further. You *must* explore every button, every function, and every command, and give the sample exam a good workout.

Candidates have repeatedly had problems with the functionality of the exam interface. If you do not know how to use the exam interface, you may lose valuable time, which, in turn, could affect your score. The AICPA has now posted a notice to candidates that it is the candidate's responsibility to become familiar with the functionality, format, and directions of the exam before reporting to the testing center. Therefore, make *sure* you familiarize yourself with the sample exam. Chapter 9 and Appendix C cover helpful hints on the exam interface.

Again, on the CPA Examination Web page, follow the link for the sample tests. Depending on how your browser is set, it may be necessary to approve each of the extra downloads to get the sample exam functioning. On some computers, it loads easily; on other computers it does not. Your Internet settings must allow active-X controls and software to be loaded on your computer.

If the sample exam does not load properly, follow the instructions located on your screen. I have loaded the sample exam on at least seven computers. I have experienced success on the first try, only three out of seven times. If the sample exam doesn't load properly, it helps to print out the instruction pages. These instructions are somewhat involved, and require you to change some settings on your computer. Therefore, it is much easier if you print them out and slowly follow them step-by-step.

In addition, the new version of the sample exam may not properly load if you have an older version of the sample exam on your computer. Again, the AICPA page has instructions on how to delete the older version, so that the new sample exam can be loaded. Print these instructions and follow the guidelines step-by-step. They will show you how to delete the older version so that the new sample exam will load.

## THE CPA SAMPLE EXAM

As discussed earlier in this chapter, the AICPA has a sample exam for each section of the CPA exam: REG, AUD, FAR, and BEC. Each sample exam is a miniexam to allow you to work with the exam interface. This cannot be said emphatically enough: The sample exam is a *must do* to prepare yourself for navigating through the exam! You will actually be able to take five multiple-choice questions, use the calculator and spreadsheet functions, enter formulas and values, make journal entries, and use the research infobase. The sample exam is invaluable for familiarizing yourself with an abbreviated version of the exam and an abbreviated version of the infobases on the exam. Spend some time and click on everything. Enter values that don't make sense and see if you get an error message. Cut and paste. Use the spell-checker. Try every function several times and make sure it works.

An important point to make is that the entire infobase is *not* accessible in the sample exam. Because the infobases are quite large, the sample exam uses a limited set of standards to allow candidates to practice with the research interface. Don't worry, though; the sample exam infobase is still large enough to give you plenty of practice navigating and searching. However, the sample exam is not large enough to help you learn the contents of the infobases.

You will find the exam interface may do some strange things. For example, a CPA candidate and I were practicing research on the FAR sample exam. We had difficulty highlighting and transferring a research answer. After reading the instructions more carefully, we learned that the screen must be split to highlight or transfer an answer. When we performed a keyword search, we were stuck in the search and couldn't get out of it. With the FARS CD, you use arrow keys to go back or move between searches. On the CPA interface, the commands do not work the same as the commercial product. We tried to generate other searches. In order to start over, we had to clear the previous search or click on "Home." We wasted at least five or ten minutes with this. Finally, we were so frustrated that we clicked on Home. Remember, this is *not* ten minutes you want to waste on the actual CPA exam!

Keep in mind, I had read all of the tutorials and instructions, and I still had trouble. You will find that some of these instructions don't "stick" in your brain until you actually do it. So, make sure you give those sample exams a good workout! We'll cover a little more about the exam interface in Chapter 9 and Appendix C.

## IMPORTANT WEB SITES

The AICPA Web site and the FASB Web site are important to visit on a regular basis prior to taking the exam. The AICPA Web site will post any updates to the exam, and the FASB Web site will post information on new accounting pronouncements. Remember that a new pronouncement is testable six months after the effective date, unless early application is permitted. If early application is permitted, the standard is testable six months after the issue date. Therefore, it is important to visit the FASB and AICPA Web sites to stay current with the most recent information and literature. Make *sure* you visit these important Web sites while preparing for the CPA Exam.

The AICPA Web site has several important documents and information posted. A "must read" for all CPA candidates is the *CPA Candidate Bulletin*. The *CPA Candidate Bulletin* has information about how to apply, how to schedule the exam, what to bring to the exam, and how to prepare for the exam. The *CPA Candidate Bulletin* is found under "Getting Started" at the CPA Examination Web page. Another valuable document is the Uniform CPA Examination Content Specifications. These content specifications can be found under "Learning Resources" in "How to Prepare."

CPA Candidates should also check for any announcements or updates before taking the exam. An important source of information for updates can be found at the AICPA exam Web site under the headings "Latest News" and "Breaking News." In addition, the "Uniform CPA Examination Alert" will outline any changes to the exam and post any issues or changes regarding functionality of the exam.

Below are the addresses for Web sites that you will find valuable in preparing for the CPA exam.

| | |
|---|---|
| **AICPA Web sites** | www.aicpa.org |
| | www.cpa-exam.org |
| **FASB Web site** | www.fasb.org |
| **PCAOB Web site** | www.pcaob.org |
| **Tax Web sites** | www.irs.gov |
| | www.law.cornell.edu/uscode/html/uscode26 |

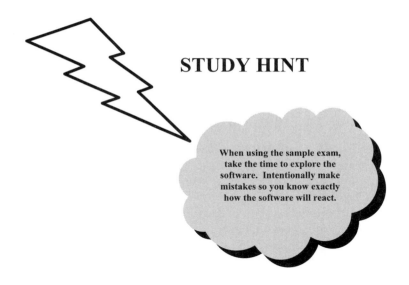

## STUDY HINT

When using the sample exam, take the time to explore the software. Intentionally make mistakes so you know exactly how the software will react.

## TEST YOURSELF

**1.** How many parts of the CPA exam test research skills?
  a.  One.
  b.  Two.
  c.  Three.
  d.  Four.

**2.** Which infobase appears on the AUD portion of the CPA exam?
  a.  Financial Accounting and Reporting System (FARS).
  b.  AICPA Professional Standards.
  c.  Internal Revenue Code.
  d.  All of the above.

**3.** Which infobase appears on the FAR portion of the CPA exam?
  a.  Financial Accounting Research System (FARS).
  b.  AICPA Professional Standards.
  c.  Internal Revenue Code.
  d.  All of the above.

**4.** Which section of the CPA exam may require more than one research task on a simulation?
  a.  FAR.
  b.  REG.
  c.  AUD.
  d.  BEC.

**5.** Where can you find Publication 17?
  a.  The FASB Web site.
  b.  The AICPA Web site.
  c.  The SEC Web site.
  d.  The IRS Web site.

**6.** The FASB Statements are available in which format?
  a.  Paper copy.
  b.  At the FASB Web site.
  c.  FARS CD.
  d.  FARS Online.
  e.  All of the above.

**7.** The FASB Statements located at the FASB Web site are searchable by keyword.
  a.  True.
  b.  False.

**8.** The financial accounting standards are continually updated and edited for changes at the FASB Web site.
  a.  True.
  b.  False.

**9.** Publication 17 contains information on deductions, exclusions, and limits for certain deductions.
  a.  True.
  b.  False.

**10.** The AICPA provides the CPA candidate with resources and infobases to practice all three areas of research before the CPA exam.
  a.  True.
  b.  False.

# 2 FINANCIAL ACCOUNTING RESEARCH SYSTEM (FARS)

Once you have access to the financial accounting literature, it is important to understand the similarities and differences of the versions of the literature. This chapter will examine the organization and structure of the hard copy of the standards, the FARS CD infobase, and the FARS Online infobase. Chapters 3 and 4 will expand our coverage and provide a more detailed look at the contents of various types of pronouncements. First, let's focus on the general organization of the authoritative literature for financial accounting.

## PRINTED VERSIONS OF THE LITERATURE

As discussed in Chapter 1, the printed version of the authoritative literature is published by the Financial Accounting Standards Board. The book version of the accounting standards can be purchased online from John Wiley & Sons, Inc. or ordered from your local bookstore. In addition, a paper copy of an accounting standard can be downloaded in .pdf format from the FASB Web site at www.fasb.org. Several differences exist between the printed textbook version and the online version of the standards.

The paper version of the standards published in book form has a topical index in the back of the book. Superseded material is shaded in gray. Amended material is identified with a black line to the left of the text, and the new text may be inserted and underlined. Superseded and amended paragraphs are also identified in the "Affected by" heading at the beginning of the standard. The book version is updated once each year.

The downloadable version of the literature found at the FASB Web site is the actual standard exactly as it appeared when the standard was issued. In other words, the .pdf version has not been updated or annotated for superseded or amended material. Because the .pdf versions of the older financial accounting literature at the FASB Web site are not current, these original standards have limited usefulness for studying for the CPA exam. However, the FASB Web site is extremely helpful for studying the most recently issued standards.

As indicated in the *CPA Candidate Bulletin*, a standard is testable six months after the effective date. However, if early application is permitted, a standard is testable six months after the issue date. Therefore, candidates should always visit the FASB Web site and check for any new pronouncements issued since the publication of their CPA Review materials.

### ORGANIZATION AND STRUCTURE OF FARS INFOBASES

The financial accounting literature is also published in two computerized formats: FARS CD and FARS Online. Both the FARS CD and the FARS Online versions of the literature are referred to as "infobases" because these products are a database of information. Both the FARS CD and the FARS Online version of the infobases are updated each year and annotated for changes. In addition, the computerized versions of the literature are searchable by keywords. The content of the FARS CD is similar to the content of FARS Online. The major differences between these two products are the menus, search commands, navigation, retrieval of records, and display of results.

Both the FARS CD and FARS Online infobases contain seven topical areas. The infobases resemble the printed version of the standards. The computerized infobases contain the following components:

1. Original Pronouncements
2. Original Pronouncements as Amended
3. Current Text
4. EITF Abstracts
5. Implementation Guides
6. Derivative Instruments and Hedging Activities
7. Topical Index

Only the first six items contain information. The seventh item, Topical Index, is the alphabetical index that is cross-referenced to both the Original Pronouncements and Current Text. A word of caution here: Although the topical index is cross-referenced and has links in both the Original Pronouncements and Current Text, it should be considered a crutch in research. It is not a substitute for familiarizing yourself with the infobase in preparing for the CPA exam. In fact, relying on the topical index to begin a search may result in a candidate spending too much time on a research question.

The FARS CD version also contains a FARS Reference Guide. This reference guide contains instructions for various commands in the infobase. Its contents are unique to the commercial infobase that uses Folio for navigation.

The FARS Online version of the infobase also has instructions on how to use it. The instructions for FARS Online are found by clicking on a link on the left-hand side of the main menu labeled "How to Use FARS."

As you know, the CPA exam is a closed exam, and the contents are not to be disclosed by any individual taking the exam. Therefore, candidates must rely on the information provided by the AICPA as to the contents of the exam and which infobases could be tested in research.

At this time, it appears the research questions on the FAR portion of the CPA exam are limited to answers that can be found in the Original Pronouncements and Current Text. Therefore, the acceptable research answers can be cited from either the Original Pronouncements or the Current Text. A candidate must decide which of these to use because only one answer is allowed. Let's explain the differences in these two sources.

## The Original Pronouncements

The Original Pronouncements (OPs) contain all of the financial accounting standards promulgated by the Committee on Accounting Procedures (CAP), the Accounting Principles Board (APB), and the Financial Accounting Standards Board (FASB). All of the pronouncements are in chronological (date) order. The oldest pronouncements are first. The most recent pronouncements are last. Therefore, when you open the original pronouncements, you will find the Accounting Research Bulletins (ARBs), then the Accounting Principles Board Opinions (APBs), and then the Statements of Financial Accounting Standards (SFAS, or more commonly called FAS), in that order.

The Original Pronouncements include ALL accounting pronouncements issued; therefore, both the superseded and amended pronouncements can be found in the OPs. Superseded material is shaded in gray, and amended material has a black line to the left of the text. There is usually a red diamond, called a jump link, that takes the reader, or "jumps," from the superseded or amended material to the updated material.

The Original Pronouncements are also in another form, "as Amended." In the commercial version of the infobase, the Original Pronouncements as Amended are the original pronouncements that have been edited and updated for changes.

It appears that the CPA exam is using a special version of the Original Pronouncements as Amended. However, on the CPA sample exam, superseded material has not been completely deleted. If the material is superseded, it should be shaded in gray. If the standard has been amended, the CPA sample exam infobase appears to have included the changes and incorporated any amendments into the text.

An important point to remember when working with the Original Pronouncements is this: Never cite superseded material! A candidate would waste valuable time reading superseded material. If the paragraph is shaded in gray, you have reached a dead end, and you should not be using that as your answer. Move on!

Citations from the Original Pronouncements contain the standard number and the paragraph number. For example, the following are citations of the various standards.

ARB 43, par. 9
APB 12, par. 4
FAS 5, par. 6

The paragraph number is useful in understanding *where* you are in the standard. For example, if the citation indicates the researcher is in FAS 133, par. 394, the reader is either near the end of a very long standard, or perhaps the reader is in the appendix. As a general rule, the appendices to standards usually contain examples, clarifications, or dissenting opinions. It is unlikely you would be required to cite information from an appendix, since the CPA exam should be looking for the general rule, which is found in the body of the standard.

## The Current Text

The Current Text is organized and numbered differently from the Original Pronouncements. The Current Text contains the general standards, industry standards, and current text passages that are superseded but are still applicable due to delayed effective dates. Other than that, the Current Text, as implied by its name, is current. Therefore, the only superseded material found in the Current Text is when a new FASB statement has been recently issued, and it is that brief period of time when both standards are allowed. After the effective date, the current text is updated to reflect only the standard that applies.

General standards are used by all companies. Industry standards are specialized standards for a particular industry, such as the recording industry, banking industry, or the motion picture industry. You may see only the general standards on the CPA exam, or you may see both the general and industry standards.

## The EITF Abstracts & Implementation Guides

EITF Abstracts are the full text of the issues discussed by the Emerging Issues Task Force since its formation in 1984. The FASB created the EITF to address new issues and problems in practice that the existing standards do not address. The Implementation Guides contain Special Reports and FASB Staff Positions.

## USING FARS ON THE CPA EXAM

In practice, an accountant needs all of these standards for research. However, at this point, not all parts of the infobase are accessible or tested on the exam. Currently, the AICPA has included the Original Pronouncements as Amended and the Current Text portions of the infobase on the FAR exam. As the CPA Exam evolves over time, the AICPA may choose to expand the infobases to include more testable components. For right now, it is best to be comfortable with the Original Pronouncements as Amended and the Current Text.

When you open the authoritative literature on the CPA exam, you should find two links: the Original Pronouncements as Amended (OPs) and the Current Text (CT). Clicking on one source will limit your keyword search to that portion of the infobase. Another way to limit your search is to select a particular standard or group of standards (ARBs or APBs), and perform a "search within." Therefore, if you are using a keyword search, you can search both the Original Pronouncements and the Current Text simultaneously. Searching the OPs and the CT at the same time sounds fabulous, but it is both good and bad. It's good because it is a comprehensive search; it's bad because it provides far too many results to read. I've heard horror stories of how candidates wasted 30 minutes on the CPA exam doing keyword searches and reading results. You don't have that kind of time. So, let's focus on learning our way around!

## OVERVIEW OF THE ORIGINAL PRONOUNCEMENTS

The Original Pronouncements contain all the accounting pronouncements of the Committee on Accounting Procedures (CAP), the Accounting Principles Board (APB), and the Financial Accounting Standards Board (FASB) in chronological (date) order. It is important to note that a chronological order is often key to finding older versus more recent issues. We'll take a historical look at which topics are old and which ones are new. We'll also take a structural look at the different kinds of pronouncements, as each type of pronouncement (ARB, APB, or FASB Statement) is organized differently.

The Original Pronouncements apply to all for-profit and not-for-profit entities. Governmental entities are covered by the pronouncements issued by the Governmental Accounting Standards Board (GASB). Governmental accounting is testable both in the multiple-choice and simulation portions of the exam. However, according to the CPA Candidate Bulletin, the AICPA has not yet included GASB standards on the research component of the exam. Only the Original Pronouncements and Current Text should be on the FAR research component of the exam.

The Original Pronouncements begin with the Accounting Research Bulletins issued by the Committee on Accounting Procedure (CAP). The Accounting Research Bulletins are abbreviated ARB. Next, you will see the Accounting Principles Board Opinions, abbreviated APB. These two, the ARBs and the APBs, include all pronouncements issued prior to the organization of the FASB in late 1973.

Next, you will find the AICPA Accounting Interpretations (AIN), Accounting Principles Board Statements (APS), and Accounting Terminology Bulletins (ATB). These Interpretations and Statements give guidance on implementing the accounting standards. It is unlikely these items will be included on the exam.

Finally, you will see the FASB Statements passed by the Financial Accounting Standards Board. The FASB Statements, also referred to as Statements of Financial Accounting Standards, or FAS, contain the most recent pronouncements issued by the Financial Accounting Standards Board. However, many of these standards have been amended or superseded. Knowing your way around the FASB Statements is crucial for quick and accurate results on the CPA exam. The Statements are abbreviated FAS for Financial Accounting Standard.

In addition to the FASB Statements, the complete FASB literature also contains the FASB Interpretations (FIN) and Technical Bulletins (FTB), as well as the Statements of Financial Accounting Concepts (CON).   FASB Interpretations attempt to clarify, explain, or elaborate on an existing FASB Statement.  As of June 1, 2007, the FARS CD infobase included 48 Inter-pretations of the FASB.  These FASB Interpretations require a two-thirds majority vote of the board members.

FASB Technical Bulletins are lower in authority than the FINs.  They do not require a vote of the FASB.  These FTBs address issues that are less controversial; therefore, the FASB Technical Bulletins may address a small number of firms.  The FASB Technical Bulletins are numbered by the year of issue with a hyphen and a number.  For example, FTB 87-2 indicates that the Technical Bulletin was the second bulletin issued in 1987.

The FASB Concept Statements are also in the infobase and are formally titled Statements of Financial Accounting Concepts (SFACs).  The SFACs or Concept Statements are the conceptual framework for accounting standards.   These are considered the lowest level of authority in the hierarchy of accounting literature.   The FASB Concept Statements are numbered 1 through 7.   A citation from the Concept Statements is abbreviated by listing the concept statement number and the paragraph number.   For example, CON6, par. 2 indicates the paragraph is from Statement of Financial Accounting Concepts 6, paragraph 2.  The Concept Statements are usually included in the Original Pronouncements; therefore, it is possible the AICPA may include the Concept Statements in the infobase on the exam.

As discussed previously, candidates are responsible for research in the Original Pronouncements and Current Text.  It is unclear whether the CPA exam will test beyond the ARBs, the APBs, and the FASB Statements on the exam.  Therefore, it's important that every candidate is aware of these lower-tiered sources such as Interpretations, Technical Bulletins, and Con-cept Statements.  Remember that any material found in these infobases can potentially be tested.

## THE HIERARCHY OF GAAP

The AICPA defined the hierarchy of GAAP in SOP 93-3.  This hierar-chy is divided into five levels of authority. The highest level of authority is category A; the lowest is Category E.  Exhibit 2.1 is a listing of the hierarchy of GAAP from the highest to the lowest level.

**Exhibit 2.1:  Hierarchy of GAAP**

| *Category* | *Pronouncement* |
|:---:|:---|
| A | FASB Statements<br>FINs by FASB<br>APB Opinions by APB<br>ARBs by CAP |
| B | FTBs by FASB<br>AICPA Industry Audit and Accounting Guides<br>AICPA SOPs |
| C | EITFs by FASB<br>AICPA AcSEC Practice Bulletins |
| D | AICPA Accounting Interpretations (AIN)<br>FASB Implementation Guides  (Q&A) |
| E | SFACs by FASB<br>AICPA Issue Papers, Technical Practice Aids |

Again, notice that the FASB Statements are the highest in priority, and the Concept Statements are the lowest in priority.

Candidates must know the contents of the accounting literature to answer questions in the multiple-choice and simulation portions of the exam. Remember, though, that candidates do *not* have access to the literature in the multiple-choice portion of the exam.  Even if the infobase were available, a candidate would not have enough time to search for answers to the multiple-choice questions.   Likewise, a candidate will not have sufficient time to search for answers on the various components of a simulation.  A candidate should not rely on the infobase to search for answers to routine questions. Research in the literature should be limited to the research question assigned on the simulation.

## THE ORIGINAL PRONOUNCEMENTS AND THE CURRENT TEXT—UNDERSTANDING THE DIFFERENCE

There is a considerable difference between the Original Pronouncements (OP) and the Current Text (CT).  First, the Original Pronouncements are just that—the original writings of the authoritative body.  The OPs are organized in numerical order.  When a new standard is issued, it is usually given the next sequential number.  Exceptions to this rule are standards that have been revised such as FAS 123(R), FAS 132(R), and FAS 141(R).  Therefore, as a general rule, the Original Pronouncements are in date or chronological order.  Older material is first, followed by newer material.  When a researcher cites something from the Original Pronouncements, it is cited by the pronouncement number and the paragraph.  For example, ARB 45, par. 7; APB

12, par. 6; or FAS 5, par. 3 are correct citations from three different types of pronouncements.

The Current Text is completely different. It is a compilation and re-wording or paraphrasing of all accounting rules contained in the authoritative literature, organized by topic. In other words, the authors of the Current Text looked everywhere in the literature to find the rules for leases (FAS 13, FAS 27, FAS 28, FAS 91, etc.), and put all the rules together under "L" for leases. The authors then assigned each rule a paragraph number in the Current Text. The numbering system in the current text is a system developed by the Current Text authors. A citation from the Current Text might look something like this: C101.34, or L10.8, or D58.101. At the end of each Current Text passage, the authors use brackets to cross-reference the material to the original pronouncements.

So, if the Current Text is in alphabetical order by topic, you must be thinking, this is great! This sounds too good and too easy to be true! And you are right—it is! Sometimes finding items in the Current Text can be tricky if an individual does not use precise accounting vocabulary.

For example, I wanted to find something on deferred taxes. I thought, this is easy, I should go to "D" for deferred taxes. However, the standard is actually entitled FAS 109, Accounting for Income Taxes. Although accountants talk about deferred taxes, this topic is placed in the Current Text under "I" for income taxes, not D for deferred taxes. Another time I wanted to research treasury stock, so I looked under "T" for treasury. Again, I found nothing and was somewhat surprised. I looked further and found it under "C" for Capital Stock: Treasury Stock.

At times you will find some unusual organization with the current text. For the most part, though, it is relatively easy to locate a particular topic. A candidate should become familiar with both sources since both the OPs and the CT can be used on the exam. If you have difficulty with one source, you can move to the other source, or you can jump into the search menu and do a quick keyword search. Then you can find approximately where that topic is in the infobase, and locate it via the table of contents in either the OPs or CT if necessary.

## USING THE ORIGINAL PRONOUCEMENTS EFFICIENTLY

If you know your way around FARS, use the Original Pronouncements and go straight to the accounting pronouncement. If you don't know the accounting pronouncement, try a keyword search. If the results are overwhelming, try a new keyword search with different vocabulary. In the commercial version of the FARS CD product, you can move to the contents window to narrow down your results by looking at the titles of the pronouncements to determine if anything is "on point."

If you prefer working with the Current Text, you can start your search there. If you are totally unfamiliar with a topic, go to the Current Text and try to find the topic in the alphabetical index. If the term is not there, try a keyword search and look through the results.

The key to research is to skim quickly. Do not get bogged down trying to read everything slowly. Do not get frustrated. Try a variety of searches with different vocabulary terms and try them quickly. Skim and move on. Consider this a race against the clock. Since the entire simulation is only supposed to take 30-40 minutes, your goal is to find your research answer in FARS in four to seven minutes.

## OVERVIEW OF THE CURRENT TEXT

As we discussed earlier, the Current Text contains the general standards and industry standards. The current text is a compilation of accounting treatments that paraphrases the original pronouncements and cross-references the explanation back to the original accounting standards. At present, you can use either the Original Pronouncements or Current Text on the CPA exam.

The General Standards of the Current Text are those standards that apply to all businesses and not-for-profit entities. A brief sample of the contents of the Current Text General Standards is shown in Exhibit 2.2.

**Exhibit 2.2:  Current Text General Standards**

| Section | Title |
|---------|-------|
| A07 | Accounting Changes and Error Correction |
| A10 | Accounting Policies |
| A31 | Additional Paid-in Capital |
| A35 | Adjustments of Financial Statements for Prior Periods |
| B05 | Balance Sheet Classification:  Current Assets and Current Liabilities |
| B10 | Balance Sheet Display: Offsetting |
| B51 | Business Combinations |
| C08 | Capital Stock:  Capital Transactions |
| C11 | Capital Stock: Dividends-in-Kind |
| C16 | Capital Stock: Preferred Stock |
| C20 | Capital Stock: Stock Dividends and Stock Splits |
| C23 | Capital Stock: Treasury Stock |
| C24 | Capital Structure Disclosures |
| C29 | Changing Prices: Reporting Their Effects in Financial Reports |
| C32 | Commitments:  Long-Term Obligations |
| C35 | Compensation: Share-Based Payments |
| C39 | Compensation to Employees: Deferred Compensation Agreements |
| C44 | Compensation to Employees: Paid Absences |

Open your infobase and examine the full table of contents of the Current Text closely. Now let's make some interesting observations. First, the numbered list is not complete. For example, the numbers jump from A07 to A10 to A31 with nothing in between. Second, the numbering system is completely different from the Original Pronouncements. The Current Text begins each section's number with the section and then a decimal point and three digits. For example, A07.101. The decimal numbers begin at .101 in each section and are numbered consecutively, (i.e. A07.101, A07.102, A07.103, and so forth).

The glossary or definitions are located in a 400 series toward the end of the section. The glossary for accounting changes and error corrections begins at A07.401. The glossary section is important because it contains definitions of items. For example, the glossary in A07.401 defines an accounting change and clarifies that a correction of an error is not an accounting change. The glossary, therefore, may contain information on a specific accounting rule. It may also paraphrase rules and definitions that are normally found in the early paragraphs of a FASB Statement.

As discussed earlier, an important feature of the Current Text is that the table of contents or index is not a complete list of all vocabulary items, issues, or accounting topics. As we discussed previously, treasury stock is not on the topic list. Instead, it is found in C08, Capital Stock: Treasury Stock. Another example is that F60 is described as Foreign Currency Translations. However, this section also contains information on foreign currency transactions. You may find that using the table of contents in the Current Text requires a bit of imagination and use of different vocabulary terms to find what you need. If you decide to use the Current Text on the exam, you should study the table of contents and become familiar with its organization. When using the Current Text on the exam, if you don't see what you need quickly, try another search strategy—perhaps a keyword search or a search within would work best.

## A CLOSER LOOK AT THE ORIGINAL PRONOUNCEMENTS

If you choose to use the Original Pronouncements for research on the CPA exam, you should become familiar with its contents and organization before the exam. Finding information in the Original Pronouncements is easier if you know what is old and what is new, and if you understand exactly how the standard is organized. Each type of standard, the ARBs, the APBs, the older FASB Statements, and the newer FASB Statements, are organized differently. Let's look at each type of standard.

### What's Old and What's New

Generally, the simpler, noncontroversial transactions are found in the earlier standards. Items like inventory, depreciation, current assets, and current liabilities are found in the ARBs. The ARBs begin in June 1953 and end in August 1959. They are numbered ARB 43 through 51. In earlier years, business transactions were not as complex as today. Therefore, the accounting was more straightforward and basic issues were covered by the ARBs. Notice that ARB 43 is an important pronouncement because it restated and revised the older Accounting Research Bulletins.

The APBs are the Accounting Principles Board Opinions. The APBs begin with APB 1 in November 1962 and end with APB 31 in June, 1973. Although the APBs are relatively old and many of the APB Opinions are superseded, the APBs still in effect contain some of our older and important accounting rules.

The FASB Statements begin in December 1973. There has been some criticism that accounting suffers from accounting standards overload (too many accounting standards). Yes, it's true; as of January 2008, there are 160 FASB Statements. However, changes in the environment of business have necessitated new standards to address newer, more creative transactions.

Good news! Much of the ARB and APB material is superseded, and many of the older FASB statements are no longer in effect. The next two chapters will focus on the most important material to know in each of these sections. For now, let's examine the structure of each type of pronouncement or standard. The structure of each type of standard is very different. If you understand how the particular type of standard is organized, you will find your answer more quickly.

## THE STRUCTURE OF THE ARBS, APBS, AND FASB STATEMENTS

### The ARBs

The first accounting research bulletin, ARB 43, is special because it revised and restated previous accounting research bulletins. ARB 43 begins with a long introduction. After the introduction, there are 15 chapters covering various accounting topics. Unfortunately, the content layout does not follow a uniform pattern in each chapter.

Some chapters are divided into **Sections** such as Section A and Section B. Other chapters in ARB 43 identify the rule by **Statement,** such as "Statement 1," and then follow with a discussion. When researching, you should look for the appropriate rule that is usually located in the statement (not the discussion). The discussion following the statement provides examples and explanations.

Other ARBs do not use the term **Statement**. Instead, these ARBs begin by outlining the accounting definitions and rules paragraph by paragraph. Generally, the order of these paragraphs is a brief explanation of the standard, the definitions, and the accounting treatment. Be sure not to quote the explanation as the accounting rule.

## The APBs

The APBs are organized differently from the ARBs. In general, they follow a pattern, as shown in Exhibit 2.3.

**Exhibit 2.3: Organization of APB Opinion**

| **APB Opinions** |
| --- |
| Introduction |
| Definitions |
| Applicability |
| Discussion |
| Opinion |
| Effective date |

As a researcher, you will probably be most interested in the definitions, the applicability (the scope or type of items to which the rules apply), and the opinion. Although the discussion section might further clarify the scope and the application of the principle, the actual rule is contained in the opinion paragraph(s). Be careful to cite the opinion and *not* the discussion if you are asked for an accounting rule.

## The FASB Statements

The older FASB Statements are slightly different from the newer FASB statements. The older Statements usually have five components, as shown in Exhibit 2.4.

**Exhibit 2.4:  Organization of the Older FASB Statements**

| **FASB** Statements |
| --- |
| Summary (brief) |
| Introduction |
| Standards |
| Disclosures |
| Effective date and transition |

In these older standards, the introduction might contain definitions. Also, the scope should appear in the earlier material. Some of the statements have a summary at the beginning. The accounting rules are located under "Standards." The disclosures section is where financial statement presentation and footnote disclosure rules are located. The effective date and transition includes rules on converting to the new standard.

The more recent FASB pronouncements are much more structured. It appears this change occurred with FAS 141 in 2001. New statements issued after 2001 include a larger amount of background material, a summary, and an introduction.   The summary contains a section that explains the reasons for issuing the statement, differences between the new statement and the previous statements, how it improves financial reporting, how it relates to the conceptual framework, and the effective date and transitioning requirements.   Although this is excellent background reading for learning a particular accounting standard, a candidate should not be spending valuable time on the CPA exam reading these summaries.   Candidates should know their way around the statements and be able to find the rule.   The newer statements usually contain the following components as shown in Exhibit 2.5.

**Exhibit 2.5:  Organization of the Newer FASB Statements**

| |
|---|
| **Recent FASB Statements** |
| Summary |
|     Reasons for issuing this statement |
|     Differences between this statement and previous statement |
|     How the changes in this statement improve financial reporting |
|     How conclusions in this statement relate to the conceptual framework |
| Introduction |
| Standards of financial accounting & reporting |
|     Scope |
|     Definitions |
|     Accounting rules |
|     Disclosures |
|     Effective dates and transition |
| Appendices |

Let's look at each part of the newer FASB Statements.  As discussed earlier, the summary and introduction are very conversational and easy to understand.  Often, the summary and introduction explain the accounting treatment.  This part of the standard is excellent to read if you need to build vocabulary or understand a rule.  However, the summary and introduction are *not* the rules.  The rules are found under "Standards."

The **Standards** are precisely that—the accounting standards!  On the newer FASB pronouncements, these standards will be organized in a special order: scope, definitions, rules, disclosures, effective dates, and transition requirements.

The **scope** identifies what is covered by the standard and what is not covered by that standard.  For example, FAS 142 (goodwill and other intangibles) explains in the scope that FAS 142 applies to intangible assets acquired individually or in a group of other assets, but NOT intangibles acquired in a business combination. Further research will show that intangibles acquired in a business combination are covered by FAS 141.  It is important to understand the scope of the pronouncement to understand what types of transactions are covered by the rules. If an item is not covered in the scope of that standard, the researcher is in the wrong standard. Move on!

The **definitions** are usually found after the scope and near the beginning of the pronouncement. It is important to understand the definition to make sure the item in question fits within the definition. For example, in FAS 142, the Statement provides rules for intangible assets and goodwill. However, the Statement further defines that although goodwill is considered an intangible asset, for purposes of FAS 142, an intangible asset is any intangible *other* than goodwill. Be careful to read definitions.

The **accounting rules** include rules related to valuation, allocation to periods, classification issues, netting rules, etc. In your infobase on the CPA exam, you will see the accounting rules for FASB statements in an outlined list. If you were to look at a hard copy of the accounting standards, the titles of these "documents" in the infobase will be the bolded headings within each standard. This book will discuss the importance of infobase structure in Chapter 8. The CPA exam interface is covered in Chapter 9.

**Disclosures** refer to both financial statement disclosures and footnote disclosures. Disclosures may include rules for presentation on the balance sheet, income statement, statement of cash flows, or statement of owners' equity. Disclosures will also include additional disclosures required in the notes to the financial statements (footnote disclosures).

**Effective dates and transition** explain when the standard becomes effective and any special transition or disclosure rules for changing to the new standard.

The Appendices to the FASB Statement provide background information and examples on how to apply the standard. Of course, the amount of support material to explain the pronouncement varies with the complexity of the pronouncement. FAS 141(R) is my personal favorite with approximately 32 pages of text in the standard itself, but a whopping 312 pages of appendices!

## WHY THE STRUCTURE OF THE STANDARDS IS IMPORTANT

Knowing the structure of the standards is important because if the CPA exam asks a question regarding a footnote disclosure, you should be reading for information near the *end* of the FASB standard. If the CPA exam question involves a definition, you should be looking near the *beginning* of the standard for your answer. And if the question asks about how to value a particular transaction or how to calculate an amount, you should be looking in the FASB standard *after* the scope and definitions—somewhere in the middle of the standard. If you are working with older literature, such as the APB Opinions, you know that the rule is in the Opinion paragraph.

With your knowledge about the structure of the standards, what is old and new, and quick-skimming techniques, you should be able to find your answer much more quickly.   No candidate should spend valuable time reading the entire standard.   In addition, knowing your way around the standards will keep you from feeling lost or overwhelmed during the exam.   It can also keep you from wasting time reading irrelevant material.   And, it definitely builds confidence and increases your chances of having a correct answer in a short amount of time!

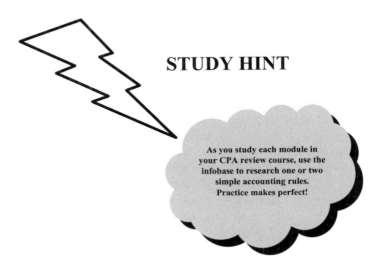

**STUDY HINT**

As you study each module in your CPA review course, use the infobase to research one or two simple accounting rules. Practice makes perfect!

## TEST YOURSELF

**1.** The Original Pronouncements as Amended have superseded material shaded in gray.
    a.    True.
    b.    False.

**2.** A CPA candidate can find the answer more quickly by searching both the Original Pronouncements and the Current Text simultaneously.
    a.    True.
    b.    False.

**3.** The FASB Web site contains the updated standards with additions and changes.
    a.    True.
    b.    False.

**4.** The FASB Concept Statements are considered the highest level of authoritative literature for GAAP.
    a.    True.
    b.    False.

**5.** Which of the following is included in Category A in the hierarchy of Generally Accepted Accounting Principles?
    a.    SFACs.
    b.    ARBs.
    c.    AICPA Interpretations.
    d.    AICPA SOPs.

**6.** Which of the following contains the oldest accounting standards?
    a.    APBs.
    b.    FASB Statements.
    c.    AICPA SOPs.
    d.    ARBs.

**7.** Which of the following standards has an Opinion paragraph that contains the accounting rules?
    a.    ARBs.
    b.    APBs.
    c.    FASB Statements.
    d.    AICPA Professional Standards.

**8.** Which of the following parts of a FASB Statement identifies what types of transactions are covered by the statement?
    a.    Definitions.
    b.    Disclosures.
    c.    Scope.
    d.    Accounting rules.

**9.** If you wanted to research the footnote disclosures required for deferred taxes, where would you most likely find this information?
    a.    At the beginning of FAS 109.
    b.    In the middle of FAS 109.
    c.    At the end of FAS 109.
    d.    In the appendix of FAS 109.

**10.** Which of the following citations is found in the Current Text?
    a.    F10.108.
    b.    ARB 43, par. 7.
    c.    FIN 35, par. 3.
    d.    FAS 5, par. 12.

# 3 FARS: THE ARBS AND THE APBS

As you can see, the FARS infobase is quite large. Now let's talk about the contents of the FARS infobase. In this chapter, we'll cover the ARBs and APBs. In Chapter 4, we'll continue our coverage of FARS and examine the FASB Statements.

## THE ACCOUNTING RESEARCH BULLETINS

The Committee on Accounting Procedure (CAP) was formed in 1939 by the AICPA (formerly referred to as the American Institute of Accountants) to address accounting issues. Between September 1939 and January 1953, CAP issued 42 Accounting Research Bulletins (ARBs). The original ARBs were numbered ARB 1 through ARB 42. In June 1953, the ARBs were revised and restated. The restatement was entitled ARB 43, *Restatement and Revision of Accounting Research Bulletins*. Therefore, the ARBs that remain in the authoritative literature today begin in 1953 and end in 1962. These newer ARBs are numbered ARB 43 through ARB 51. Let's begin our discussion with an overview and analysis of ARB 43.

### ARB 43—The Restatement and Revision

ARB 43 is a long standard that deserves special attention. ARB 43, issued in 1953, is the restatement and revision of the *Accounting Research Bulletins*. ARB 43 originally contained 15 chapters. However, a great deal of this material is completely superseded. Exhibit 3.1 outlines the titles for ARB 43 and briefly lists the contents of relevant chapters. We'll focus only on the chapters with accounting rules that are still in effect.

Although ARB 43 appears lengthy and overwhelming, we can quickly list the topics that remain in effect today. Other chapters, such as Chapters 5, 6, 8, 13, 14, and 15, are completely superseded. In addition, some items in the current chapters are either amended or partially superseded. Study Exhibit 3.1. Then open your database and look at these chapters to familiarize yourself with the content that remains in effect. Just scroll through ARB 43 quickly.

As you study, focus on vocabulary. In the professional literature, vocabulary is always changing. Think of how our society has become more politically correct in its vocabulary usage over the years. For instance, a janitor is no longer referred to as a janitor or custodian, but as a maintenance engineer. A secretary is now referred to as an administrative assistant.

**Exhibit 3.1: ARB 43: Restatement and Revision of ARBs**

| Chapters Remaining in Effect (As of May 2008) | | |
|---|---|---|
| *Chapter* | *Topic* | *Explanation of Contents* |
| 1 | Prior Opinions | This chapter restates six rules dealing with revenue recognition, unrealized profits, earned surplus, profit or loss on treasury stock, and notes receivable from officers and employees |
| 2 | Forms of Statements | Comparative financial statements are discussed here |
| 3 | Working capital | Definitions of current assets and liabilities |
| 4 | Inventory pricing | Definitions, cost flows, valuation of inventory |
| 7 | Capital Accounts | Quasi-reorganizations or corporate re-adjustments, stock dividends, and stock split-ups |
| 9 | Depreciation | Depreciation issues |
| 10 | Taxes | Real and personal property taxes, and liability for property taxes |
| 11 | Government Contracts | Cost-plus contracts, renegotiation, and termination of contracts |

The same phenomenon has happened to accounting vocabulary. The vocabulary in accounting has changed over time to adjust to the changing business environment. For example, several methods for calculating depreciation include salvage value. We now refer to salvage value as residual value. Terms such as intrinsic value were borrowed from other disciplines, such as finance. In other instances, new terms, such as projected benefit obligation or accumulated benefit obligation were created and defined by new accounting standards.

In the older accounting standards, such as ARB 43, the vocabulary can be considerably different. Familiarity of these older terms is essential for conducting research. For example, in ARB 43, retained earnings are referred to as "earned surplus." Net income or net loss is referred to as "profit" or "loss." Stock splits are referred to as "stock split-ups." As you skim through the infobase, pay particular attention to the older versus the newer vocabulary. Recognizing these differences will help you generate keyword searches to find the research answer more quickly.

Some readers might be wondering, "What is superseded in ARB 43?" First, Chapter 5 on intangibles is superseded (FAS 142 has the new rules). Chapter 6 on contingency reserves is gone (FAS 5 is new). Chapter 8 on income taxes is replaced by FAS 109. Chapter 12 on foreign operations and foreign exchange is almost entirely superseded by FAS 52. Chapter 13 on compensation for pension plans and stock compensation is completely superseded by several other pronouncements. Chapter 14 on long-term leases of lessees is superseded by FAS 13. And Chapter 15 on unamortized discounts, issue costs, and redemption premiums on bonds refunded is superseded by several other pronouncements.

Let's quickly review the most important aspects of ARB 43. The most important topics in ARB 43 are current assets and liabilities, inventory, capital accounts, depreciation, and property taxes. How do you remember this? These are very old topics, very simple topics, and not very controversial topics. Remember that the more difficult, technical, and complex topics are covered in later pronouncements.

Stop here and recite to yourself the basic older material in ARB 43 before moving on to other ARBs. Read the last paragraph at least three more times!

## The Other ARBs

Let's look at the remaining ARBs. Exhibit 3.2 outlines the remaining ARBs. As you can see, most of the ARBs have been superseded. The most important items here are construction accounting in ARB 45 and material in ARB 51 on intercompany transactions and consolidated financial statements.

**Exhibit 3.2: List of Accounting Research Bulletins—ARB 44–51**

| Number | Topic | Explanation of Contents |
|---|---|---|
| ARB 44 | Declining-Balance Depreciation | Superseded |
| ARB 44 (Revised) | Declining-Balance Depreciation | Superseded |
| ARB 45 | Long-Term Construction-Type Contracts | Percentage of Completion Method and Completed Contract |
| ARB 46 | Discontinuance of Dating Earned Surplus | Amendment to quasi-reorganization material in ARB 43 |
| ARB 47 | Accounting for Costs of Pension Plans | Superseded |
| ARB 48 | Business Combinations | Superseded |
| ARB 49 | Earnings Per Share | Superseded |
| ARB 50 | Contingencies | Superseded |
| ARB 51 | Consolidated Financial Statements | Intercompany transactions, and combined statements rules remain in effect. FAS 141 and FAS 141(R) supersedes some passages. FAS 160 supersedes other passages. |

Although most people might believe that FAS 141, FAS 141(R), and FAS 160 superseded all other material on business combinations, this is not the case. The rules for eliminating intercompany transactions and preparing combined financial statements is old material located in ARB 51. In addition, FAS 141(R) and FAS 160 have delayed effective dates. Therefore, the rules for minority interests found in ARB 51 are still in effect until the effective date of FAS 160 (fiscal years beginning after December 15, 2008). Make a mental note of that.

To review again, the ARBs are not very difficult, and your research is limited to older topics in the ARBs from 1953 through 1962. Let's take one more look at a revised ARB study list in Exhibit 3.3.

**Exhibit 3.3: Accounting Research Bulletin Study List**

| *Number* | *Topic* | *Explanation of Contents* |
|---|---|---|
| ARB 43 | Restatement and Revision of ARBs | Prior Opinions, Forms of Statements, working capital, inventory pricing, capital accounts, depreciation, property taxes, government contracts |
| ARB 45 | Long-Term Construction-Type Contracts | Percentage of completion method and completed contract |
| ARB 46 | Discontinuance of Dating Earned Surplus | Amendment to quasi-reorganization material in ARB 43 |
| ARB 51 | Consolidated Financial Statements | Intercompany transactions, minority interests (until effect date of FAS 160), and combined statements in effect. FAS 141 supersedes remaining items. FAS 160 will supersede minority interests for fiscal years beginning after December 15, 2008. |

That's it! Four ARBs are all that you need to study. Remember that ARB 43 is the longest, though, with multiple chapters. Now we will move forward with the remaining pre-FASB pronouncements, the APBs.

## THE ACCOUTING PRINCIPLES BOARD OPINIONS

The Accounting Principles Board Opinions (APBs) are numbered from 1 to 31. The first opinion, APB 1, was issued in November 1962. The last APB opinion, APB 31, was issued in June 1973. Exhibit 3.4 is a complete list of the APB Opinions. Notice that approximately half of these APB Opinions are superseded. The superseded opinions are shaded in gray.

**Exhibit 3.4: Accounting Principles Board Opinions**

| Number | Topic |
|---|---|
| APB 1 | New Depreciation Guidelines and Rules |
| APB 2 | Accounting for the "Investment Credit" |
| APB 3 | The Statement of Source and Application of Funds |
| APB 4 | Accounting for the "Investment Credit" |
| APB 5 | Reporting of Leases in Financial Statements of Lessee |
| APB 6 | Status of Accounting Research Bulletins |
| APB 7 | Accounting for Leases in Financial Statements of Lessors |
| APB 8 | Accounting for the Cost of Pension Plans |
| APB 9 | Reporting the Results of Operations |
| APB 10 | Omnibus Opinion—1966 |
| APB 11 | Accounting for Income Taxes |
| APB 12 | Omnibus Opinion—1967 |
| APB 13 | Amending Paragraph 6 of APB Opinion No. 9, Application to Commercial Banks |
| APB 14 | Accounting for Convertible Debt and Debt Issued with Stock Purchase Warrants |
| APB 15 | Earnings per Share |
| APB 16 | Business Combinations |
| APB 17 | Intangible Assets |
| APB 18 | The Equity Method of Accounting for Investments in Common Stock |
| APB 19 | Reporting Changes in Financial Position |
| APB 20 | Accounting Changes |
| APB 21 | Interest on Receivables and Payables |
| APB 22 | Disclosure of Accounting Policies |
| APB 23 | Accounting for Income Taxes—Special Areas |
| APB 24 | Accounting for Income Taxes—Investments in Common Stock Accounted for by the Equity Method |
| APB 25 | Accounting for Stock Issued to Employees |
| APB 26 | Early Extinguishment of Debt |
| APB 27 | Accounting for Lease Transactions by Manufacturer or Dealer Lessors |
| APB 28 | Interim Financial Reporting |
| APB 29 | Accounting for Nonmonetary Transactions |
| APB 30 | Reporting the Results of Operations—Discontinued Events and Extraordinary Items |
| APB 31 | Disclosure of Lease Commitments by Lessees |

The APB Opinions that remain in effect contain many amendments. They are found between the old ARBs and the FASB Statements. Therefore, you will see amendments from two directions. Some of the APBs amended the older ARBs. Then some of the FASB Statements amended the APBs and the ARBs. It is important to understand how newer standards amended the older standards. On the CPA exam, candidates should be using the Original Pronouncements as Amended. Therefore, it is possible to find certain answers in two locations in the infobase if a newer pronouncement amended an older pronouncement.

In some instances, a newer pronouncement changes or rewrites an entire sentence or paragraph. For example, FAS 153 entitled *Exchanges of Non-monetary Assets* amended APB 29, *Accounting for Nonmonetary Trans-actions.* FAS 153 rewrote APB 29, paragraph 20 by striking out the sentence and completely replacing the sentence. If you are using the Original Pronouncements as Amended, the change has already been made to APB 29 to reflect this update. Therefore, the same sentence is found in both APB 29 and FAS 153. This redundancy may appear confusing to a novice user of FARS, but the well-prepared CPA candidate will be aware of them in the accounting literature.

Take time to examine Exhibit 3.4 closely. Read the list slowly and carefully. Examine each title. Much like the old ARBs, many of the APB Opinions are also superseded. Now let's delete the superseded items and look at the list again. Exhibit 3.5 shows only the APB Opinions that remain in effect.

**Exhibit 3.5: APB Opinions in Effect as of January 2008**

| Number | Topic |
|--------|-------|
| APB 2 | Accounting for the "Investment Credit" |
| APB 4 | Accounting for the "Investment Credit" |
| APB 6 | Status of Accounting Research Bulletins |
| APB 9 | Reporting the Results of Operations |
| APB 10 | Omnibus Opinion—1966 |
| APB 12 | Omnibus Opinion—1967 |
| APB 13 | Amending Paragraph 6 of APB Opinion No. 9, Application to Commercial Banks |
| APB 14 | Accounting for Convertible Debt and Debt Issued with Stock Purchase Warrants |
| APB 18 | The Equity Method of Accounting for Investments in Common Stock |
| APB 21 | Interest on Receivables and Payables |
| APB 22 | Disclosure of Accounting Policies |
| APB 23 | Accounting for Income Taxes—Special Areas |
| APB 26 | Early Extinguishment of Debt |
| APB 28 | Interim Financial Reporting |
| APB 29 | Accounting for Nonmonetary Transactions |
| APB 30 | Reporting the Results of Operations—Discontinued Events and Extraordinary Items |

Again, carefully read the titles of the APB Opinions in Exhibit 3.5. Look at the list again and notice the special interest items. Let's make a new study list that omits the special interest items such as the investment tax credit and the APB opinions for commercial banks. Exhibit 3.6 is our new study list of the most important APB Opinions.

**Exhibit 3.6: APB Opinions Study List**

| Number | Topic |
|--------|-------|
| APB 6 | Status of Accounting Research Bulletins |
| APB 9 | Reporting the Results of Operations |
| APB 10 | Omnibus Opinion—1966 |
| APB 12 | Omnibus Opinion—1967 |
| APB 14 | Accounting for Convertible Debt and Debt Issued with Stock Purchase Warrants |
| APB 18 | The Equity Method of Accounting for Investments in Common Stock |
| APB 21 | Interest on Receivables and Payables |
| APB 22 | Disclosure of Accounting Policies |
| APB 26 | Early Extinguishment of Debt |
| APB 28 | Interim Financial Reporting |
| APB 29 | Accounting for Nonmonetary Transactions |
| APB 30 | Reporting the Results of Operations—Discontinued Events and Extraordinary Items |

It is important to examine each of these APB Opinions more thoroughly. There are some *very* important items remaining in these APBs. As we review each standard, we will also discuss some of the linkages with the newer FASB statements. Many of these APBs have paragraphs that are superseded or amended by the FASB Statements.

## A DETAILED LOOK AT THE APBs

### APB 6—Status of ARBs

Interestingly enough, the AICPA actually had a question from this one on the sample exam. What is in this old standard that is interesting? Notice that the title is not descriptive. A researcher relying on table of contents drop-down menus would not realize the information contained in APB 6. Yet, APB 6 is full of interesting information. First, APB 6 contains the rules for retirement of treasury stock, handling a gain from the sale of treasury stock, and allocating treasury stock to capital surplus. (Notice that APB 6 does not refer to "additional paid-in capital" but uses the term "capital surplus." Old vocabulary!) APB 6 also sets the rules for presentation of certain items, such as unearned discount, in the current assets and current liabilities section of the balance sheet. APB 6 further requires that finance charges or interests on the face of amount of receivables should be deducted from the receivables. APB 6 also contains the all-important rule that plant, property, and equipment should not be written up above cost. A CPA candidate should spend 10 to 15 minutes reading this standard to become familiar with the range of topics and the older vocabulary. APB 6 contains many rules that are difficult to find.

## APB 9—*Reporting the Results of Operations*

APB 9 outlines the reporting requirements for presenting the "results of operations," more commonly referred to as the Income Statement, or Statement of Operations in today's jargon. APB 9 identifies rules for displaying extraordinary items and prior period adjustments on the income statement. Be aware of two important linkages: Some of the material on extraordinary items is affected by APB 30. Material on prior period adjustments has been superseded by FAS 16 and FAS 154.

## APB 10—*Omnibus Opinion*

The APB Opinions contain two of these Omnibus "catchall" amendment-type pronouncements. One of these is almost entirely superseded; the other is *full* of important detailed information. APB 10 is the opinion that is mostly superseded. APB 10 contains an amendment to ARB 43 Chapter 1A on installment accounting. This rule is easily found by using a keyword search, and ARB 43 should be appropriately amended. If the candidate encounters a research question about installment accounting, ARB 43 should be updated to include the changes. The remainder of APB 10 is superseded, so we'll delete it from our study list.

## APB 12— *Omnibus Opinion*

APB 12 is the omnibus act that is *full* of important rules and changes. Again, the title of this pronouncement does not give the reader a clue as to its contents.

APB 12 outlines the presentation of allowance accounts on the financial statements, the footnote disclosures required for depreciation, accounting for deferred compensation to employees or surviving spouses, the required disclosures for the statement of owners' equity (number of shares, changes in each account, etc.), and how to amortize a discount or premium (the calculation, not the disclosure).

APB 12 is the standard that requires a company to deduct the allowance or contra account from the asset or group of assets to which it relates. APB 12 also requires financial statement footnotes for depreciation as to major classification of depreciable assets, accumulated depreciation by class of assets, and a description of the depreciation methods used.

A few other interesting points on APB 12: Statement of Owners' Equity was referred to in earlier years as "Statement of Capital Changes." Notice in APB 12 that the old vocabulary of "earned surplus" has evolved and is now referred to as "retained earnings." Watch out for APB 12! APB 12 is full of some important details that are difficult to find. You may want to read APB 12 once or twice to familiarize yourself with the assorted rules, so the information can be found quickly if you encounter a research question on any of these topics.

## APB 14—*Accounting for Convertible Debt and Debt Issued with Stock Purchase Warrants*

The title on this pronouncement is self-explanatory. Take a look at this pronouncement. The pronouncement contains a large amount of discussion, but the actual opinions are very brief: paragraphs 12, 16, 17, and 18. If you are on point with the correct topic, skim the standard quickly and look for the opinion paragraph. Knowing that you don't have to wade through an enormous amount of material, but simply scroll down quickly to find the opinion, will make your job much easier and faster!

Another issue in conducting research in APB 14 is vocabulary. When researching stock purchase warrants, first distinguish whether the warrant is detachable or nondetachable. Then, generate the appropriate keywords to find your answer. If you use the words *detachable warrant* in a keyword search, you will immediately find the opinion paragraph that is relevant. However, if you use the terms *nondetachable warrant*, you will find a paragraph with a dissent, which is close. Oddly enough, you would have to type in the terms *not detachable warrant* to find the opinion paragraph with the appropriate answer.

On some infobases the keyword search works easily. On other infobases, it does not retrieve the appropriate information. For example, when you type in the word *not* in the advanced query on the FARS CD, the software recognizes it as a Boolean operator. Therefore, you must put the word *not* in quotes so the program recognizes the term as a specific word search in the database and not a Boolean operator. Tricky! I hope a researcher would not encounter this problem on the search engine for the CPA exam. However, the point to stress is that every search engine is unique in the way it searches and retrieves results. In fact, sometimes using keyword searches complicates finding certain accounting rules. More on that issue later in Chapters 8 and 9!

## APB 18—*The Equity Method of Accounting for Investments in Common Stock*

Again, the title of APB 18 is self-explanatory. Some important definitions (investor, investee, subsidiary, control) are listed at the beginning of the pronouncement. The definitions of cost and equity methods are described in the discussion. The Opinion in par. 17 outlines the 20% rule and significant influence. The standard goes further to describe how to apply the equity method.

Beware of the linkage of APB 18 with FAS 115 and 159. FAS 115 is entitled *Accounting for Certain Investments in Debt and Equity Securities.* This title is descriptive because if a company owns less than 20% and does not have significant influence, the rules of FAS 115 apply. Therefore, FAS 115 only applies to "certain" investments.

Another linkage exists with FAS 159. Although FAS 159 did not amend or change APB 18 or FAS 115, FAS 159 allows a company to elect the fair value option for reporting financial assets. Therefore, if a company elects the fair value option, the rules contained in APB 18 will not apply. If you encounter a research question on valuation of investment securities, be sure to read the question carefully to determine the percentage of ownership and whether APB 18, FAS 115, or FAS 159 applies.

### APB 20—Superseded by FAS 154

APB 20 has been removed from our study list, but this standard merits discussion. APB 20 is completely superseded by FAS 154. There is no longer a cumulative effect in change of accounting method displayed on the income statement. As you know, changes in accounting principle now receive retrospective application to the earliest period presented. Make sure you are current with FAS 154!

### APB 21—*Interest on Receivables and Payables*

APB 21 is *super* important! In addition, APB 21 has information that is difficult to find if you don't know where to look. Make *sure* you read this statement in its entirety and familiarize yourself with its contents. APB 21 contains the rules for effective interest, amortization, and presentation of receivables and payables on the balance sheet.

First, the title to APB 21 is deceptive. Yes, it covers interest on receivables and payables, but it does so much more! APB 21 is also the statement that explains how to value notes exchanged for cash, property, goods, or services. It tells how to determine the interest rate, how to amortize a premium (links to APB 12 here), and how to present the discount or premium on the face of the financial statements.

Another comment is vocabulary: Although everyone in accounting uses the term "effective interest method," the statement here uses the term "interest method." Therefore, in a keyword search, this pronouncement is difficult to find if the keywords *"effective interest method"* are used instead of *"interest method."* Make a mental note of that!

### APB 22—*Disclosure of Accounting Policies*

Again, APB 22 is another *super* important standard. APB 22 is the standard that requires companies to make accounting policy disclosures for items such as inventory, depreciation, and revenue recognition. APB 22 outlines the content and format of accounting policy disclosures.

As you will see in later pronouncements, each pronouncement will include any additional footnote disclosures required for that topic. The rules for footnote disclosures are usually found near the end of the FASB statement. We'll discuss that in more detail later in this book.

The AICPA released several multiple-choice sample exam questions that require a candidate to understand the difference between accounting policy disclosures and accounting footnote disclosures. Make sure you know the difference between disclosure of accounting policies and additional disclosures in notes to the financial statements. "Policies" is the key operating word here. Read APB 22 closely to understand this important distinction, as well as the types of accounting policy disclosures required.

### APB 26—*Early Extinguishment of Debt*

This opinion is only relevant to the debtor. It defines net carrying amount, reacquisition price, and requires recognition of gain or loss on the extinguishment of debt. Creditor rules have been superseded and are found in FAS 114.

### APB 28—*Interim Financial Reporting*

APB 28 has the basic rules for interim financial reporting. However, you need to be careful here. As new FASB statements are issued, the newer standard may provide guidance or include disclosure requirements for interim reporting for that specific topic. The newer interim reporting requirements for specific topics can be found toward the end of each new FASB standard.

### APB 29—*Accounting for Nonmonetary Transactions*

This opinion covers nonmonetary transactions, but it has some very important changes made by FAS 153. The distinction of similar versus dissimilar assets no longer exists, and is replaced by a new requirement that the transaction either has commercial substance or lacks commercial substance. This distinction affects whether the transaction is recorded at fair value or book value. APB 29 has very important linkages with the new FAS 153—make sure you don't miss these. Keep in mind, though, the CPA exam uses the Original Pronouncements as Amended, so any changes and new vocabulary should already be incorporated into APB 29 or linked to APB 29. However, you may find the answer in two locations in the infobase.

**APB 30—*Reporting the Results of Operations: Discontinued Events and Extraordinary Items***

Another *super important* opinion!  First, all of the material on discontinued operations has completely been superseded by FAS 144.  The rules for reporting discontinued operations are now in the back of FAS 144, *Accounting for the Impairment or Disposal of Long-lived Assets,* which is not very intuitive to find.  Second, the definition of extraordinary is in APB 30: infrequent and unusual.  Third, the treatment of extraordinary items is also found in APB 30.  Finally, the treatment of an item that is unusual or infrequent but not both is also addressed in APB 30.  APB 30 also provides a list of items that are *never* considered extraordinary.

The research issue of early extinguishment of debt is somewhat more complicated.  FAS 4 amended APB 30 and made early extinguishment of debt an extraordinary item.  Then FAS 145 rescinded FAS 4, which means that early extinguishment of debt is no longer routinely considered extraordinary.  This rule is difficult to find because FAS 145 is one of those "catch-all" pronouncements that amends a variety of other pronouncements.  FAS 145 links back to FAS 4, which in turn links back to APB 30. This is difficult to find because it is in FAS 145, titled *Amendments to Existing Pronouncements to Reflect Rescission of Statements 4, 44, and 64.*  FAS 145 merely listed this change as a deletion of a phrase or sentence of a previous pronouncement.  FAS 145 does not overtly state in any of the sentences that early extinguishment of debt is no longer extraordinary.  Instead you have to read between the lines and find the deletion.  Do you feel like you are going in circles here?  Absolutely!  However, if you are aware of certain problem areas in the standards, you can avoid wasting valuable time on the CPA exam.  I would hope that the amended infobase is nicely cross-referenced to avoid this type of confusion.  However, be sure to know where this is, just in case you encounter a research question, because it is difficult to find.

As we said earlier, the CPA exam should be using the amended version of the database.  Hopefully, these standards will be updated for any of these amendments.  It's nice to know where the redundancies exist because you may find two different answers that look very similar.  You certainly don't want to feel like you are going in circles!  If you feel that you are reading information that is redundant, look at the cross-referencing.  It is probably an amendment, and either citation would be an acceptable answer.

## NEW APB STUDY LIST

Perhaps the APBs seem overwhelming, but let's put together a quick study list and examine the list in its entirety.  Our new study list is shown in Exhibit 3.7.

The good news is that the APBs, like the ARBs, contain some of the more established, older accounting pronouncements.  Most of the titles are fairly explicit with the exception of APB 6, 12, and 21.  Therefore, you can rely on the titles of most of the pronouncements to search for your accounting issue. However, be sure to study APB 6, APB 12, and APB 21 in depth to make *sure* you can find the detailed gems located within. Remember that the rules for notes receivable, notes payable, and interest are all hiding in APB 21.

**Exhibit 3.7: APB Opinions Quick Study List**

| Number | Title | Topics |
|---|---|---|
| APB 6 | Status of Accounting Research Bulletins | Retirement of Treasury stock; Gain on sale of Treasury Stock; Discounts on receivables; PPE not to be written up above cost |
| APB 9 | Reporting the Results of Operations | Extraordinary items at bottom of I/S, link to APB 30 Prior period adjustments, link to FAS 16 |
| APB 12 | Omnibus Opinion—1967 | Disclosure of allowance accounts Footnote disclosures depreciation Deferred compensation Disclosures in Statement of O.E. Amortization of discount/ premium |
| APB 14 | Accounting for Convertible Debt and Debt Issued with Stock Purchase Warrants | Convertible debt Stock purchase warrants |
| APB 18 | The Equity Method of Accounting for Investments in Common Stock | 20% rule, significant influence, control Cost method, equity method |
| APB 21 | Interest on Receivables and Payables | Notes exchanged for cash, property, goods or services; determining interest rate; amortization of discounts and premiums; "Interest method"; statement presentation of premiums and discounts |
| APB 22 | Disclosure of Accounting Policies | Accounting policy disclosures |
| APB 26 | Early Extinguishment of Debt | Calculations and gain/loss for debtor |
| APB 28 | Interim Financial Reporting | Interim financial statements |
| APB 29 | Accounting for Nonmonetary Transactions | Exchange of nonmonetary assets, link to FAS 153 for amendment for commercial substance rules |
| APB 30 | Reporting the Results of Operations—Discontinued Events and Extraordinary Items | Extraordinary Items Discontinued Operations now in FAS 144 |

## PUTTING IT ALL TOGETHER

It makes sense that outlining accounting policies, footnote disclosures, basic presentation of information on the income statement were promulgated earlier in the history of US accounting standards. Remember, most of the basic rules and disclosures for topics such as inventory, depreciation, the classified balance sheet, the multistep income statement, and footnotes are in the older materials: the ARBs and the APBs. Now we will move into the newer, more specialized FASB Statements!

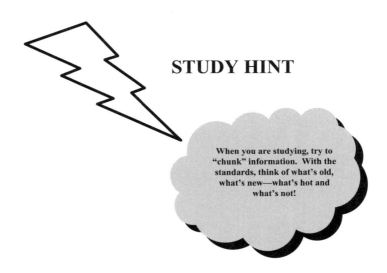

**STUDY HINT**

When you are studying, try to "chunk" information. With the standards, think of what's old, what's new—what's hot and what's not!

## TEST YOURSELF

**1.** Approximately how many *Accounting Research Bulletins* are in the authoritative literature that have not been superseded?
    a.   One.
    b.   Four.
    c.   Ten.
    d.   Twenty-two.

**2.** In which area of APB 18 will you find the accounting rules for how to record income for an investee in which the company owns more than 30% of the outstanding stock?
    a.   Discussion.
    b.   Introduction.
    c.   Definitions.
    d.   Opinion.

**3.** Two Omnibus Opinions are included in the APB Opinions. Which of the following standards are the Omnibus Opinions?
    a.   APB 10 and 12.
    b.   APB 21 and 41.
    c.   APB 30 and 42.
    d.   APB 21 and 22.

**4.** Which standard outlines the accounting rules for extraordinary items?
    a.   APB 22.
    b.   APB 29.
    c.   APB 30.
    d.   APB 6.

**5.** Which accounting standard outlines the disclosures of accounting policies?
    a.   APB 6.
    b.   ARB 43.
    c.   ARB 51.
    d.   APB 22.

**6.** In which standard will you find the definitions of current assets and current liabilities?
    a.   APB 18.
    b.   ARB 43.
    c.   ARB 51.
    d.   APB 21.

**7.** In which standard will you find the rules for the debtor for early extinguishment of debt?
    a.   ARB 43.
    b.   ARB 51.
    c.   APB 6.
    d.   APB 26.

**8.** In which area of the accounting standards will you find the rules for discontinued operations?
    a.   ARB 43.
    b.   APB 6.
    c.   APB 30.
    d.   FAS 144.

**9.** Beach Company owns 35% of the stock of Costa Corporation and can exercise significant influence. Beach Company elects the fair value method for reporting its investment in Costa. Which standard would contain the appropriate accounting rules to value the stock of Costa?
    a.   ARB 43.
    b.   APB 18.
    c.   FAS 115.
    d.   FAS 159.

**10.** Gemstone Corporation repurchased 100 shares of its stock and subsequently resold those shares at a gain of $7 per share. Which accounting standard would identify the rules for accounting for the gain on the sale of the Gemstone stock?
    a.   ARB 43.
    b.   ARB 45.
    c.   APB 6.
    d.   APB 21.

## PRACTICE YOUR RESEARCH SKILLS

Find the appropriate citation from the ARBs and the APBs to answer each of the following questions.

1. Can the loss on disposal of a segment or component of a business be recorded as an extraordinary loss?

2. What is the definition of a current asset?

3. What is an extraordinary item?

4. What information regarding depreciation must be disclosed?

5. What is a stock split?

6. What is the definition of a current liability?

7. How does a company value a small stock dividend?

8. How should allowance for uncollectible accounts be disclosed in the financial statements?

9. Inventory is sometimes required to be stated at lower of cost or market. Define the term lower of cost or market as it relates to inventory valuation.

10. How does a company determine if a transaction has commercial substance in a non-monetary exchange?

# 4 THE FASB STATEMENTS

At first, studying the list of FASB statements can be overwhelming. As of January 1, 2008, there were 160 FASB Statements. Studying the FASB Statements is easier if we analyze them and put them in a better context. To make studying easier, we will group the FASB Statements, or the Financial Accounting Standards (FAS), in chunks of 50. We will examine FAS 1–50, FAS 51–100, and FAS 101–150. Then we'll look at the most recent statements, FAS 151–160.

First, we will shade everything in gray that is superseded. Then we will delete the statements that are "special interest" and not likely to be tested on the exam. This will leave a core set of pronouncements that you need to review for each grouping. At the end of this chapter, the standards most likely to be tested will be included in one comprehensive study list.

## HOW TO STUDY THE STANDARDS

After working on several projects and doing research in the standards, I have noticed some interesting aspects about the standards. When the FASB issues a new pronouncement, I think of the new pronouncement as falling into one of three categories:

- Creates a new set of rules for a specific topic or issue
- Amends one pronouncement
- Amends several pronouncements

This distinction is useful in remembering the particular pronouncement.

When the FASB issues a new, clear-cut, comprehensive set of accounting rules on one topic, I refer to this as a stand-alone pronouncement. These stand-alone pronouncements are easy to remember because they usually address fairly large, important issues. Stand-alone pronouncements are easy to find because the title of the standard clearly identifies the topic. On the CPA exam, these stand-alone pronouncements are easy to find by using the drop-down menus in the table of contents. Unfortunately, in our previous material with the ARBs and APBs, few stand-alone pronouncements exist, making this area of research more challenging. Examples of stand-alone pronouncements in the FASB statements are FAS 5, *Accounting for Contingencies,* FAS 95, *Statement of Cash Flows,* and FAS 128, *Earnings Per Share.*

A second distinction to make when analyzing the standards is the type of pronouncement that amends only one other pronouncement. A new standard that amends only one earlier pronouncement is also easy to locate because the nature of the amendment is usually in the title. For example, FAS 149 is entitled *Amendment of FASB Statement No. 33 on Derivatives and Hedging Activities.* Obviously, FAS 149 amends the rules on derivatives found in FAS 133.

The third distinction in the types of standards is the type of pronouncement that either covers several topics or amends and modifies several previous standards. I refer to these as "catchall" type pronouncements because they are catching all of the loose ends, addressing minor issues, and making clarifications on several topics or existing pronouncements. A new standard that amends several pronouncements is much more challenging to remember. For example, FAS 145 supersedes and amends a variety of rules for unrelated topics in several pronouncements. These catchall standards are more difficult to remember, and the titles are not always clear.

The APB Omnibus Opinions, discussed in Chapter 3, are examples of these catchall type pronouncements, wherein the title is not reflective of the contents. A researcher must actually read the entire standard and make a mental note of its contents. In addition, a researcher must rely more on keyword searches to find issues in these catchall standards.

A good study strategy for the CPA candidate is to rely on the titles of the standards and know the approximate location of the stand-alone pronouncements (earlier standards versus later standards). For catchall standards, a candidate should be aware of the contents of certain pronouncements, such as ARB 43, APB 12, and APB 21. For catchall amendments, the candidate may be able to rely on the annotated or amended version of the infobase. As discussed in earlier chapters, the CPA exam should be using the "as amended" version of the standards. Therefore, the catchall amendments should have the changes incorporated into the appropriate standard, but the answer will be found in two places.

Let's analyze the standards more closely and learn the location of the most important standards.

## GROUPING THE STANDARDS FOR STUDY

### FAS 1–50

To give a historical perspective, the list includes the year the standard was issued. The first 50 standards were issued from 1973 to 1981. They are shown in Exhibit 4.1. Note that superseded standards are shaded in gray.

**Exhibit 4.1: FASB Statements 1–50**

| Date | Number | Title of Standard |
|------|--------|-------------------|
| 1973 | FAS 1 | Disclosure of Foreign Currency Translation Information |
| 1974 | FAS 2 | Accounting for Research and Development Costs |
| | FAS 3 | Reporting Accounting Changes in Interim Financial Statements |
| 1975 | FAS 4 | Reporting Gains and Losses from Extinguishment of Debt |
| | FAS 5 | Accounting for Contingencies |
| | FAS 6 | Classification of Short-Term Obligations Expected to Be Refinanced |
| | FAS 7 | Accounting and Reporting by Development Stage Enterprises |
| | FAS 8 | Accounting for the Translation of Foreign Currency Transactions and Foreign Currency Financial Statements |
| | FAS 9 | Accounting for Income Taxes—Oil and Gas Producing Companies |
| | FAS 10 | Extension of "Grandfather" Provisions for Business Combinations |
| | FAS 11 | Accounting for Contingencies—Transition Method |
| | FAS 12 | Accounting for Certain Marketable Securities |
| 1976 | FAS 13 | Accounting for Leases |
| | FAS 14 | Financial Reporting for Segments of a Business Enterprise |
| 1977 | FAS 15 | Accounting by Debtors and Creditors for Troubled Debt Restructurings |
| | FAS 16 | Prior Period Adjustments |
| | FAS 17 | Accounting for Leases—Initial Direct Costs |
| | FAS 18 | Financial Reporting for Segments of a Business Enterprise—Interim Financial Statements |
| | FAS 19 | Financial Accounting and Reporting by Oil and Gas Producing Companies |
| | FAS 20 | Accounting for Forward Exchange Contracts |
| 1978 | FAS 21 | Suspension of the Reporting of Earnings Per Share and Segment Information by Nonpublic Enterprises |
| | FAS 22 | Changes in the Provisions of Lease Agreements Resulting from Refundings of Tax-Exempt Debt |
| | FAS 23 | Inception of the Lease |
| | FAS 24 | Reporting Segment Information in Financial Statements That Are Presented in Another Enterprise's Financial Report |
| 1979 | FAS 25 | Suspension of Certain Accounting Requirements for Oil and Gas Producing Companies |
| | FAS 26 | Profit Recognition on Sales-Type Leases of Real Estate |
| | FAS 27 | Classification of Renewals or Extensions of Existing Sales-Type or Direct Financing Leases |
| | FAS 28 | Accounting for Sales with Leasebacks |

| Date | Number | Title of Standard |
|---|---|---|
| | FAS 29 | Determining Contingent Rentals |
| | FAS 30 | Disclosure of Information about Major Customers |
| | FAS 31 | Accounting for Tax Benefits Related to U.K. Tax Legislation Concerning Stock Relief |
| | FAS 32 | Specialized Accounting and Reporting Principles and Practices in AICPA SOPs and Audit and Accounting Guides |
| | FAS 33 | Financial Reporting and Changing Prices |
| | FAS 34 | Capitalization of Interest Cost |
| 1980 | FAS 35 | Accounting and Reporting by Defined Benefit Pension Plans |
| | FAS 36 | Disclosure of Pension Information |
| | FAS 37 | Balance Sheet Classification of Deferred Income Taxes |
| | FAS 38 | Accounting for Preacquisition Contingencies of Purchased Enterprises |
| | FAS 39 | Financial Reporting and Changing Prices: Specialized Assets—Mining and Oil and Gas |
| | FAS 40 | Financial Reporting and Changing Prices: Specialized Assets—Timberlands and Growing Timber |
| | FAS 41 | Financial Reporting and Changing Prices: Specialized Assets—Income-Producing Real Estate |
| | FAS 42 | Determining Materiality for Capitalization of Interest Cost |
| | FAS 43 | Accounting for Compensated Absences |
| | FAS 44 | Accounting for Intangible Assets of Motor Carriers |
| 1981 | FAS 45 | Accounting for Franchise Fee Revenue |
| | FAS 46 | Financial Reporting and Changing Prices: Motion Picture Films |
| | FAS 47 | Disclosure of Long-Term Obligations |
| | FAS 48 | Revenue Recognition When Right of Return Exists |
| | FAS 49 | Accounting for Product Financing Arrangements |
| | FAS 50 | Financial Reporting in the Record and Music Industry |

FAS 1–50 is a long list. It definitely feels overwhelming! Read this list slowly and carefully. As you read, mentally note which standards are superseded. Then read the list again and make a mental note of the items that appear to be special interest topics. Now, let's examine a new study list with the superseded items and special topics deleted.

You are probably wondering—why not print the shorter list to study right away? Why is it important to see the entire list with superseded items?

First, you should not try to memorize lists. CPA candidates already have an enormous amount of material memorized for the exam. In the research area, it is better if you have an overview and awareness of the standards. Seeing the infobase in its entirety provides a stronger overview. If a researcher knows approximately where certain standards are located within the literature, the accounting rules are more easily retrieved. Therefore, it is not necessary to know exactly where something is. If you know the approximate location, you can easily locate the topic or issue using the table of contents or a keyword search.

Second, the Original Pronouncements infobase contains superseded topics. It helps to know exactly how much material must be bypassed when searching the infobase. Of course, the CPA exam is a closed exam. Therefore, it is not clear whether the research component on the CPA exam will utilize the entire infobase, or just a selected portion in each of the testing areas. To be safe and prepare for any research topic, studying with the entire contents of the infobase intact is preferable.

After you have carefully read the list of titles in FAS 1–50, it is time to narrow the study list. First, everything that is superseded will be deleted. Then, let's reduce the list further by eliminating the "special interest standards" for certain industries such as banking, railroad, oil and gas, mining, savings and loans, record companies, stage companies, and television, insurance companies, broadcasters, regulated companies, and not-for-profit. After superseded and special interest topics are deleted, the list is considerably shorter. Exhibit 4.2 identifies the remaining standards from FAS 1–50 that you should study for the exam.

**Exhibit 4.2: FAS 1–50, Quick Study List**

| *Number* | *Title of Standard* |
|---|---|
| FAS 2 | Accounting for Research and Development Costs |
| FAS 5 | Accounting for Contingencies |
| FAS 6 | Classification of Short-Term Obligations Expected to Be Refinanced |
| FAS 13 | Accounting for Leases |
| FAS 15 | Accounting by Debtors and Creditors for Troubled Debt Restructurings |
| FAS 16 | Prior Period Adjustments |
| FAS 23 | Inception of the Lease |
| FAS 27 | Classification of Renewals or Extensions of Existing Sales-Type or Direct Financing Leases |
| FAS 28 | Accounting for Sales with Leasebacks |
| FAS 29 | Determining Contingent Rentals |
| FAS 34 | Capitalization of Interest Cost |
| FAS 35 | Accounting and Reporting by Defined Benefit Pension Plans |
| FAS 37 | Balance Sheet Classification of Deferred Income Taxes |
| FAS 42 | Determining Materiality for Capitalization of Interest Cost |
| FAS 43 | Accounting for Compensated Absences |
| FAS 45 | Accounting for Franchise Fee Revenue |
| FAS 47 | Disclosure of Long-Term Obligations |
| FAS 48 | Revenue Recognition When Right of Return Exists |
| FAS 49 | Accounting for Product Financing Arrangements |

Most of these titles are very descriptive. Notice that five of the standards in the list pertain to leasing. Make a mental note that FAS 13 is the *big* pronouncement on capital leases. FAS 13 is the standard where all of the definitions and rules are set for capital leases. An important point to know regarding FAS 13 is that this particular standard is divided into two parts: one part is for the lessee and the other part is for the lessor. All of the basic definitions are in the front of the pronouncement, (i.e. capital lease, bargain purchase option, guaranteed residual value, unguaranteed residual, etc.). After the definitions are listed, the standard discusses the rules for lessees. After the rules for lessees, the standard lists the rules for lessors. Beware! If you encounter a research question on leases, make *sure* to answer the question for the correct person in the problem: either the lessee or the lessor.

Historically, there has been some criticism with the FASB's rule-based approach to accounting standards. Some individuals refer to the proliferation of standards as standards overload—too many standards. One area where there is a proliferation of standards is accounting for leases. Notice that this list includes several (five) pronouncements that address leasing issues.

For example, FAS 13 addressed accounting for leases. After the standard was issued, other issues surfaced that FAS 13 failed to address. Therefore, we have FAS 23 that deals with the inception of the lease, FAS 27 on classification of renewals or extension of leases, FAS 28 on accounting for sales with leasebacks, and FAS 29 on contingent rentals. Although you do not need to memorize these standard numbers, you do need to be aware that these linkages exist. If you know they exist, you can use the drop-down menu to find the titles quickly. In the next chapter, we'll take special care to identify these linkages for you.

Another set of linkages to notice in FAS 1–50 is that this area of the standards has three standards that relate to debt: FAS 6, 15, and 47. Again, debt and disclosures of debt have been historically messy issues. No one likes debt, no one likes disclosing debt, and certainly no one likes disclosing short-term debt!

Notice that FAS 6 addresses the classification of short-term debt if it is expected to be refinanced. These rules address the requirement for classification of an item to long-term debt—the intent to refinance and the ability to consummate the refinancing. Then we have FAS 15 for troubled debt restructurings. FAS 15 is only for the debtor, as the creditor side is now dealt with by FAS 114. Also, notice that the old terminology for the debtor is *troubled debt restructuring*; the new vocabulary today for the creditor is *loan impairment*.

Another important issue regarding debt is the footnote disclosure requirements that are found in FAS 47. The beginning of the pronouncement focuses on long-term purchase obligations. Near the end of the pronouncement, you'll find the rules for long-term debt disclosures and sinking fund disclosures for each of the next five years and in the aggregate. This rule is important and it's difficult to find. Know where to find this.

FAS 37 deserves a special comment. FAS 37 addresses the rules for classifying deferred taxes on the balance sheet. At one point, FAS 37 was superseded. Then FAS 109 was issued, and since it did not conflict with the rules in FAS 37, the FASB reinstated FAS 37. FAS 37 provides that deferred tax assets or deferred tax liabilities should be classified as current or noncurrent based on the classification of the related asset or liability. It also states that if there is no associated asset or liability, then you should classify deferred tax assets or liabilities by the expected reversal date.

But, you are probably thinking, didn't FAS 109 overtly state these classification rules? Yes, Yes, Yes—FAS 109, par. 41 certainly did! And FAS 109, par. 42 has the netting rules for you. So, even though FAS 37 is still in effect, let's delete FAS 37 from our Quick Study List. Everything on deferred taxes can be found in FAS 109, and FAS 37 is redundant.

A second standard to point out before deleting it from our quick study list is FAS 35. This is the accounting and reporting for the actual pension plan itself. Don't get this confused with the employer accounting for pensions. But know it's there, just in case you should get a question. FAS 35 has the rules for the pension plan. FAS 87 has the rules for the employer who contributes to the plan. To shorten our study list to the most testable standards, we'll omit FAS 35.

Finally, you should commit to memory several important issues in these early FASB Statements. Statements 1–50 have some very important pronouncements. FAS 5 on contingencies is important: remember the probable, possible, remote? Then we have the big rule on research and development: what is research and what is not. The rules for expensing R&D are in FAS 2. Capitalization of interest is also here in FAS 34, with a little amendment made by FAS 42. Let's delete FAS 42 from our quick study list, because if you are using the amended pronouncements, it should be cross-referenced for you.

Notice that some problem areas involving revenue recognition were resolved during this era. The FASB did a nice job with certain revenue recognition issues. Franchise revenue is in FAS 45, and revenue recognition when right of return exists is in FAS 48. Think: It was important to solve these revenue recognition problems back in the earliest years of the FASB's existence.

Exhibit 4.3 is our revised Quick Study List for FAS 1–50. This list is definitely more manageable!

**Exhibit 4.3:  FAS 1–50, Quick Study List**

| Number | Title of Standards |
|--------|--------------------|
| FAS 2 | Accounting for Research and Development Costs |
| FAS 5 | Accounting for Contingencies |
| FAS 6 | Classification of Short-Term Obligations Expected to Be Re-financed |
| FAS 13 | Accounting for Leases |
| FAS 15 | Accounting by Debtors and Creditors for Troubled Debt Restructurings |
| FAS 16 | Prior Period Adjustments |
| FAS 23 | Inception of the Lease |
| FAS 27 | Classification of Renewals or Extensions of Existing Sales-Type or Direct Financing Leases |
| FAS 28 | Accounting for Sales with Leasebacks |
| FAS 29 | Determining Contingent Rentals |
| FAS 34 | Capitalization of Interest Cost |
| FAS 43 | Accounting for Compensated Absences |
| FAS 45 | Accounting for Franchise Fee Revenue |
| FAS 47 | Disclosure of Long-Term Obligations |
| FAS 48 | Revenue Recognition When Right of Return Exists |
| FAS 49 | Accounting for Product Financing Arrangements |

## FAS 51–100

Now let's look at the next set, FAS 51–100.  This covers, roughly, a period of time from 1981 to 1988.  Again, superseded items are shaded in gray.  This is an era when the FASB seemed to address problem areas for specific industries.  This grouping contains standards for the cable television industry, insurance companies, broadcasters, mortgage banking, real estate, oil and gas, banking or thrift institutions, railroads, regulated enterprises, and not-for-profit organizations.  Exhibit 4.4 outlines the titles of FAS 51–100.

**Exhibit 4.4:  FASB Statements 51–100**

| Year | Number | Title of Standard |
|------|--------|-------------------|
| 1981 | FAS 51 | Financial Reporting by Cable Television Companies |
|      | FAS 52 | Foreign Currency Translation |
|      | FAS 53 | Financial Reporting by Producers and Distributors of Motion Picture Films |
| 1982 | FAS 54 | Financial Reporting and Changing Prices: Investment Companies |
|      | FAS 55 | Determining whether a Convertible Security is a Common Stock Equivalent |
|      | FAS 56 | Designation of AICPA Guide and SOP 81-1 and SOP 81-2 as Preferable for Purposes of Applying APB Opinion 20 |
|      | FAS 57 | Related-Party Disclosures |

| Year | Number | Title of Standard |
|------|--------|-------------------|
|      | FAS 58 | Capitalization of Interest Cost in Financial Statements That Include Investments Accounted for by the Equity Method |
|      | FAS 59 | Deferral of the Effective Date of Certain Accounting Requirements for Pension Plans of State and Local Government Units |
|      | FAS 60 | Accounting and Reporting by Insurance Enterprises |
|      | FAS 61 | Accounting for Title Plant |
|      | FAS 62 | Capitalization of Interest Cost in Situations Involving Certain Tax-Exempt Borrowings and Certain Gifts and Grants |
|      | FAS 63 | Financial Reporting by Broadcasters |
|      | FAS 64 | Extinguishments of Debt Made to Satisfy Sinking-Fund Requirements |
|      | FAS 65 | Accounting for Certain Mortgage Banking Activities |
|      | FAS 66 | Accounting for Sales of Real Estate |
|      | FAS 67 | Accounting for Costs and Initial Rental Operations of Real Estate Projects |
|      | FAS 68 | Research and Development Arrangements |
|      | FAS 69 | Disclosures about Oil and Gas Producing Activities |
|      | FAS 70 | Financial Reporting and Changing Prices:  Foreign Currency Translation |
| 1983 | FAS 71 | Accounting for the Effects of Certain Types of Regulation |
|      | FAS 72 | Accounting for Certain Acquisitions of Banking or Thrift Institutions |
|      | FAS 73 | Reporting a Change in Accounting for Railroad Track Structures |
|      | FAS 74 | Accounting for Special Termination Benefits Paid to Employees |
|      | FAS 75 | Deferral of the Effective Date of Certain Accounting Requirements for Pension Plans of State and Local Government Units |
|      | FAS 76 | Extinguishment of Debt |
|      | FAS 77 | Reporting by Transferors for Transfers of Receivables with Recourse |
|      | FAS 78 | Classification of Obligations That Are Callable by the Creditor |
| 1984 | FAS 79 | Elimination of Certain Disclosures for Business Combinations by Nonpublic Enterprises |
|      | FAS 80 | Accounting for Futures Contracts |

| Year | Number | Title of Standard |
|------|--------|-------------------|
|  | FAS 82 | Financial Reporting and Changing Prices: Elimination of Certain Disclosures |
| 1985 | FAS 83 | Designation of Certain AICPA Guides and Statement of Position as Preferable for Purposes of Applying APB Opinion 20 |
|  | FAS 84 | Induced Conversions of Convertible Debt |
|  | FAS 85 | Yield Test for Determining Whether a Convertible Security is a Common Stock Equivalent |
|  | FAS 86 | Accounting for the Costs of Computer Software to Be Sold, Leased, or Otherwise Marketed |
|  | FAS 87 | Employers' Accounting for Pensions |
|  | FAS 88 | Employers' Accounting for Settlements & Curtailments of Defined Benefit Pension Plans and for Termination Benefits |
| 1986 | FAS 89 | Financial Reporting and Changing Prices |
|  | FAS 90 | Regulated Enterprises. Accounting for Abandonments and Disallowances of Plant Assets, Amendment to FAS 71 |
|  | FAS 91 | Nonrefundable Fees & Costs Associated with Originating or Acquiring Loans and Initial Direct Costs of Leases |
| 1987 | FAS 92 | Regulated Enterprises—Accounting for Phase-in Plans |
|  | FAS 93 | Recognition of Depreciation by Not-for-Profit Organizations |
|  | FAS 94 | Consolidation of All Majority-Owned Subsidiaries |
|  | FAS 95 | Statement of Cash Flows |
|  | FAS 96 | Accounting for Income Taxes |
|  | FAS 97 | Accounting by Insurance Companies for Certain Long-Duration Contracts & Realized Gains & Losses on Investment Sales |
| 1988 | FAS 98 | Accounting for Leases |
|  | FAS 99 | Deferral of the Effective Date of Recognition of Depreciation by Not-for-Profit Organizations |
|  | FAS 100 | Accounting for Income Taxes—Deferral of the Effective Date of FASB Statement No. 96 |

Once again, those 50 standards seem overwhelming. Now let's remove superseded items and special interest type items. Exhibit 4.5 shows our new Quick Study List.

**Exhibit 4.5:  FAS 51–100, Quick Study List**

| Number | Title of Standard |
|--------|-------------------|
| FAS 52 | Foreign Currency Translation |
| FAS 57 | Related Party Disclosures |
| FAS 58 | Capitalization of Interest Cost in Financial Statements That Include Investments Accounted for by the Equity Method |
| FAS 66 | Accounting for Sales of Real Estate |
| FAS 67 | Accounting for Costs and Initial Rental Operations of Real Estate Projects |
| FAS 68 | Research and Development Arrangements |
| FAS 78 | Classification of Obligations That Are Callable by the Creditor |
| FAS 84 | Induced Conversions of Convertible Debt |
| FAS 86 | Accounting for the Costs of Computer Software to Be Sold, Leased, or Otherwise Marketed |
| FAS 87 | Employers' Accounting for Pensions |
| FAS 88 | Employers' Accounting for Settlements & Curtailments of Defined Benefit Pension Plans and for Termination Benefits |
| FAS 89 | Financial Reporting and Changing Prices |
| FAS 91 | Nonrefundable Fees & Costs Associated with Originating or Acquiring Loans and Initial Direct Costs of Leases |
| FAS 94 | Consolidation of All Majority-Owned Subsidiaries |
| FAS 95 | Statement of Cash Flows |
| FAS 98 | Accounting for Leases |

This abbreviated list is definitely more manageable.  Now let's analyze this list more closely.  The FAS 51–100 era can be thought of as tying up more loose ends.  If you look closely at this list, you will find some interesting items.  The FASB still was not finished with leases.  Two more standards, FAS 91 and FAS 98, also address leasing issues.  FAS 91 addresses the initial direct costs of leases, and FAS 98 addresses issues with leases for real estate, definition of lease term, and more on initial direct costs of leases.  Then we see more on capitalization of interest:  FAS 58 and FAS 62, and more on R&D in FAS 68.  And we see more on debt in FAS 78 and 84.

The FASB continued to issue new pronouncements to address issues that were not covered by the first pronouncement on a particular issue.  Think of that as tying up any loose ends.  If we set these "loose ends" type pronouncements to the side, and look at the new *basic* pronouncements issued during this era, we see some *very* important pronouncements.  Most of these are stand-alone pronouncements and have stood the test of time with few changes and updates.  Make *sure* you can find these quickly.  The following is a list of the most important stand-alone pronouncements in this era:

| FAS 52 | Foreign Currency Translations |
| FAS 57 | Related-Party Disclosures |
| FAS 87 | Employers' Accounting for Pensions |
| FAS 95 | Statement of Cash Flows |

FAS 95 is the standard on the statement of cash flows and is very comprehensive. The FASB did a great job with this pronouncement. Almost everything about cash flows is in that standard. However, be careful to watch for standards that were issued *after* FAS 95. For example, FAS 115 changed the handling of marketable securities. We now have trading securities, available-for-sale securities, and held-to-maturity securities. When FAS 95 was issued, these distinctions and terms did not exist. Therefore, it makes perfect sense that FAS 115 must address the cash flow issues for these new terms. Look near the end of FAS 115 for amendments or changes to earlier pronouncements.

Another interesting observation from Statements 51–100 is the attempt at revising the standard for deferred income taxes. The FASB issued FAS 96, but delayed implementation. Then the FASB issued FAS 100 to delay the implementation of FAS 96. As you'll see in our coverage of the next 50 standards, the FASB delayed the implementation of the deferred tax pronouncement two more times (FAS 103 and 108), before the FASB decided to write a new standard. These extra standards delaying implementation are just used-up standard numbers that make the list look longer than it really is. FAS 109 is *Accounting for Income Taxes,* and that's the only standard you need to know for income taxes. You can ignore the other income tax standards in FAS 51–100.

## FAS 101–150

Now let's look at FAS 101–150. This is the era from 1988 to 2003. Again, everything superseded is shaded in gray. Exhibit 4.6 outlines FAS 101–150.

**Exhibit 4.6: FASB Statements 101–150**

| Year | Number | Title of Standard |
|------|--------|-------------------|
| 1988 | FAS 101 | Regulated Enterprises—Accounting for the Discontinuation of Application of FASB Statement No. 71 |
| 1989 | FAS 102 | Statement of Cash Flows—Exemption of Certain Enterprises and Classification of Cash Flows from Certain Securities Acquired for Resale |
|  | FAS 103 | Accounting for Income Taxes—Deferral of the Effective Date of FASB Statement No. 96 |
|  | FAS 104 | Statement of Cash Flows—Net Reporting of Certain Cash Receipts and Cash Payments and Classification of Cash Flows from Hedging Transactions |

| Year | Number | Title of Standard |
|---|---|---|
| 1990 | FAS 105 | Disclosure of Information about Financial Instruments with Off-Balance-Sheet Risk and Concentrations of Credit Risk |
|  | FAS 106 | Employers' Accounting for Postretirement Benefits other than Pensions |
| 1991 | FAS 107 | Disclosures about Fair Value of Financial Instruments |
|  | FAS 108 | Accounting for Income Taxes—Deferral of the Effective Date of FASB Statement No. 96 |
| 1992 | FAS 109 | Accounting for Income Taxes |
|  | FAS 110 | Reporting by Defined Benefit Pension Plans of Investment Contracts |
|  | FAS 111 | Rescission of FASB Statement No. 32 and Technical Corrections |
|  | FAS 112 | Employers' Accounting for Postemployment Benefits |
|  | FAS 113 | Accounting and Reporting for Reinsurance of Short-Duration and Long-Duration Contracts |
| 1993 | FAS 114 | Accounting by Creditors for Impairment of a Loan |
|  | FAS 115 | Accounting for Certain Investments in Debt and Equity Securities |
|  | FAS 116 | Accounting for Contributions Received and Contributions Made |
|  | FAS 117 | Financial Statements of Not-for-Profit Organizations |
| 1994 | FAS 118 | Accounting by Creditors for Impairment of a Loan—Income Recognition and Disclosures |
| 1995 | FAS 119 | Disclosure about Derivative Financial Instruments and Fair Value of Financial Instruments |
|  | FAS 120 | Accounting and Reporting by Mutual Life Insurance Enterprises and by Insurance Enterprises for Certain Long-Duration Participating Contracts |
|  | FAS 121 | Accounting for the Impairment of Long-Lived Assets and for Long-Lived Assets to Be Disposed Of |
|  | FAS 122 | Mortgage Servicing Rights |
| 1995 | FAS 123 | Accounting for Stock-Based Compensation |
| 2004 | FAS 123(R) | Share-Based Payment |
| 1995 | FAS 124 | Accounting for Certain Investments Held by Not-for-Profit Organizations |
| 1996 | FAS 125 | Accounting for Transfers and Servicing of Financial Assets and Extinguishments of Liabilities |

| Year | Number | Title of Standard |
|------|--------|-------------------|
| | FAS 126 | Exemption from Certain Required Disclosures about Financial Instruments for Certain Nonpublic Entities |
| | FAS 127 | Deferral of the Effective Date of Certain Provisions of FASB Statement No. 125 |
| 1997 | FAS 128 | Earnings Per Share |
| | FAS 129 | Disclosure of Information about Capital Structure |
| | FAS 130 | Reporting Comprehensive Income |
| | FAS 131 | Disclosures about Segments of an Enterprise and Related Information |
| 1998 | FAS 132 | Employers' Disclosures about Pensions and Other |
| 2003 | FAS 132(R) | Employers' Disclosures about Pensions and Other Postretirement Benefits—An Amendment of FASB Statements No. 87, 88, and 106 |
| 1998 | FAS 133 | Accounting for Derivative Instruments and Hedging Activities |
| | FAS 134 | Accounting for Mortgage-Backed Securities Retained after the Securitization of Mortgage Loans Held for Sale by a Mortgage Banking Enterprise |
| 1999 | FAS 135 | Rescission of FASB Statement No. 75 and Technical Corrections |
| | FAS 136 | Transfers of Assets to a Not-for-Profit Organization or Charitable Trust That Raises or Holds Contributions for Others |
| | FAS 137 | Accounting for Derivative Instruments and Hedging Activities—Deferral of the Effective Date of FASB Statement No. 133 |
| 2000 | FAS 138 | Accounting for Certain Derivative Instruments and Certain Hedging Activities—An Amendment of FASB Statement No. 133 |
| | FAS 139 | Rescission of FASB Statement No. 53 and Amendments to FASB Statements No. 63, 89, and 121 |
| | FAS 140 | Accounting for Transfers and Servicing of Financial Assets and Extinguishments of Liabilities |
| 2001 | FAS 141 | Business Combinations |
| | FAS 142 | Goodwill and Other Intangible Assets |
| | FAS 143 | Accounting for Asset Retirement Obligations |
| | FAS 144 | Accounting for the Impairment or Disposal of Long-Lived Assets |
| 2002 | FAS 145 | Rescission of FASB Statements 4, 44, and 64, Amendment of FASB Statement 13, and Technical Corrections |
| | FAS 146 | Accounting for Costs Associated with Exit or Disposal Activities |

| Year | Number | Title of Standard |
|------|--------|-------------------|
|      | FAS 147 | Acquisitions of Certain Financial Institutions—An Amendment of FASB Statements 72 and 144 and FASB Interpretation 9 |
|      | FAS 148 | Accounting for Stock-Based Compensation—Transition and Disclosure, an Amendment of FASB Statement 123 |
| 2003 | FAS 149 | Amendment of FASB Statement 133 on Derivative and Hedging Activities |
|      | FAS 150 | Accounting for Certain Financial Instruments with Characteristics of Both Liabilities and Equity |

Again, let's remove all the superseded and special interest items, and focus on the most testable standards. Notice that the more recent list of standards, FAS 101–150 is a little longer. This makes perfect sense, since these standards were promulgated between 1988 and 2003. More of these standards remain in effect than earlier standards because these standards address more recent financial reporting issues.

Let's make some important observations here. First, there is a series of relatively new pronouncements that were issued and have held up well over time. These are mostly stand-alone pronouncements that addressed a specific issue. Notice that these seem to run in a series: 114, 115, 116, 117, and 118. There's another big series 128, 129, 130, 131, 132(R), 133. Then we have another big important grouping, FAS 140, 141, 142, 143, and 144.

Mixed in with all of those are some more recent pronouncements that amended or updated other pronouncements: FAS 145, 147, 149, 150. As you'll see in our next section, FAS 151, 152, 153 also were amendment-type pronouncements. The *big* stand-alone pronouncements jump from FAS 144, to 146, and then to 154. Watch out for FAS 154. FAS 154 is the *important* pronouncement that created new rules for changes in accounting principle, changes in accounting estimate, and error correction.

Another important issue to point out in the FAS 101–150 series is that the FASB has reissued several statements with the (R) designation. Normally, the FASB pronouncements are in chronological order. However, in three cases, FAS 123(R), FAS 132(R), and FAS 141(R), the FASB reissued statements with the same number and used the (R) to denote that it is a revised standard. An interesting point about FAS 123(R) is that the FASB not only revised the standard, but the FASB also changed the name of the standard. The name changed from "Accounting for Stock-Based Compensation" to "Share-Based Payments"—quite a change!

Exhibit 4-7 is our new Quick Study List for FAS 101–150. When you study this list, think of the groupings of consecutive standards, and they'll be easier to remember.

**Exhibit 4.7:  FAS 101–150, Quick Study List**

| Number | Title of Standard |
|---|---|
| FAS 106 | Employers' Accounting for Postretirement Benefits Other than Pensions |
| FAS 107 | Disclosures about Fair Value of Financial Instruments |
| FAS 109 | Accounting for Income Taxes |
| FAS 112 | Employers' Accounting for Postemployment Benefits |
| FAS 114 | Accounting by Creditors for Impairment of a Loan |
| FAS 115 | Accounting for Certain Investments in Debt and Equity Securities |
| FAS 116 | Accounting for Contributions Received and Contributions Made |
| FAS 118 | Accounting by Creditors for Impairment of a Loan—Income Recognition and Disclosures |
| FAS 123(R) | Share-Based Payment |
| FAS 128 | Earnings Per Share |
| FAS 129 | Disclosure of Information about Capital Structure |
| FAS 130 | Reporting Comprehensive Income |
| FAS 131 | Disclosures about Segments of an Enterprise and Related Information |
| FAS 132(R) | Employers' Disclosures about Pensions and Other Postretirement Benefits—an Amendment of FASB Statements No. 87, 88, and 106 |
| FAS 133 | Accounting for Derivative Instruments and Hedging Activities |
| FAS 138 | Accounting for Certain Derivative Instruments and Certain Hedging Activities—an Amendment of FASB Statement No. 133 |
| FAS 139 | Rescission of FASB Statement No. 53 and amendments to FASB Statements No. 63, 89, and 121 |
| FAS 140 | Accounting for Transfers and Servicing of Financial Assets and Extinguishments of Liabilities |
| FAS 141 | Business Combinations |
| FAS 142 | Goodwill and Other Intangible Assets |
| FAS 143 | Accounting for Asset Retirement Obligations |
| FAS 144 | Accounting for the Impairment or Disposal of Long-Lived Assets |
| FAS 145 | Rescission of FASB Statements 4, 44, and 64, Amendment of FASB Statement No. 13, and Technical Corrections |
| FAS 146 | Accounting for Costs Associated with Exit or Disposal Activities |
| FAS 149 | Amendment of FASB Statement No. 133 on Derivative and Hedging Activities |
| FAS 150 | Accounting for Certain Financial Instruments with Characteristics of Both Liabilities and Equity |

## FAS 151–154

Finally, let's look at the most recent pronouncements, FAS 151–160 in Exhibit 4.8.

**Exhibit 4.8:  Most Recent FASB Statements FAS 151–154**

| Year | Number | Title of Pronouncement |
|------|--------|------------------------|
| 2004 | FAS 151 | Inventory Costs, an Amendment of ARB No. 43, Chapter 4 |
| | FAS 152 | Accounting for Real Estate Time-Sharing Transactions—an Amendment of FASB Statements No. 66 and 67 |
| | FAS 153 | Exchanges of Nonmonetary Assets an Amendment of APB Opinion No. 29 |
| 2005 | FAS 154 | Accounting Changes and Error Corrections—a Replacement of APB Opinion No. 20 and FASB Statement No. 3 |
| 2006 | FAS 155 | Accounting for Certain Hybrid Financial Instruments |
| | FAS 156 | Accounting for Servicing of Financial Assets |
| | FAS 157 | Fair Value Measurements |
| | FAS 158 | Employers' Accounting for Defined Benefit Pension and Other Postretirement Plans |
| 2007 | FAS 159 | The Fair Value Option for Financial Assets and Financial Liabilities |
| | FAS 141(R) | Business Combinations (Effective for fiscal years beginning after December 15, 2008.) |
| | FAS 160 | Noncontrolling Interests in Consolidated Financial Statements—an Amendment of ARB 51 Combinations (Effective for fiscal years beginning after December 15, 2008.) |

## FAS 151

FAS 151 is merely an amendment to inventory costing (old material) in ARB 43.  FAS 151 contains a clarification of the accounting rules for abnormal amounts of overhead, freight, material handling costs, and spoilage. This standard also requires that allocation of fixed overhead costs should be based on the normal capacity of the production facilities.  FAS 151 requires that abnormal amounts for these items be recognized as expense in the current period.  Since FAS 151 is an amendment to ARB 43, Chapter 4, the amended version of the infobase should reflect the updates in the older pronouncement.

## FAS 152

FAS 152 is an amendment to the accounting for certain real estate found in FAS 66 and 67.  The amendments in FAS 152 should be reflected in updated material in those standards.

## FAS 153

FAS 153 is an important amendment that attempts to bring United States accounting standards in line with international accounting standards. FAS 153 changes the wording of APB 29 on exchanges of nonmonetary transactions. It eliminates the distinction of similar versus dissimilar assets and replaces that rule with the new distinction that a transaction either has economic substance or lacks economic substance. The changes made by FAS 153 should be incorporated into the amended version of APB 29. Therefore, you may find answers to this a question on nonmonetary transactions in two places in the infobase.

## FAS 154

FAS 154 is an important pronouncement. FAS 154 is the new statement for accounting changes and error corrections. FAS 154 supersedes APB 20. Important definitions are at the beginning of the standard. Normally, footnote disclosures are found at the end of the standard. However, in FAS 154, the footnote disclosures for each item are found interwoven into the text and included at the end of each topic.

FAS 154 covers four topics: change in accounting principle, change in accounting estimate, change in reporting entity, and correction of an error in previously issued statements. These topics are found in that specific order in FAS 154. Again, the rules are listed first, and the rules for footnote disclosures are included near the end of each topic.

## FAS 155

FAS 155 is an amendment to FAS 133 and FAS 140 and covers several new rules for accounting for certain hybrid financial instruments. These amendments should be reflected in the revised text of FAS 133 on derivatives and FAS 140 on transfers and servicing of financial assets and extinguishment of liabilities.

## FAS 156

FAS 156, *Accounting for Servicing of Financial Assets,* is another amendment to FAS 133 and FAS 140. FAS 156 requires all separately recognized servicing assets and liabilities to be recorded at fair value. FAS 156 also allows an entity to choose either the amortization method or the fair value measurement method to report servicing assets and liabilities. Again, because FAS 156 is an amendment to FAS 133 and FAS 140, these new rules should be incorporated into the amended version of the previous standards.

## FAS 157

FAS 157 is a new important pronouncement that amended a long list of pronouncements. FAS 157 changed the definition of fair value. Previously, fair market value was defined in the literature as the exchange price in an arm's-length transaction between unrelated parties. FAS 157 redefined the term fair value and established a set of rules for measuring fair value. The new definition of fair value appears to slightly change the wording of the old definition, but *beware*—there are a number of other rules that explain how to identify the fair value, such as the priority of inputs of information, the market participants, and the highest and best use of the asset. FAS 157 goes further to identify how to determine fair value at date of recognition, the inputs to valuation techniques, and the fair value hierarchy of inputs.

FAS 157 requires that these new fair value measurements be applied to any other statement that requires or permits fair value measurements. However, be careful of scope limitations with FAS 157. FAS 157 does *not* apply to certain items such as FAS 123(R) *Share-Based Payments,* and inventory pricing. These scope limitations are found at the beginning of the standard. Definitions of terms are near the beginning of the standard. The accounting rules follow, and the footnote disclosure rules are at the end of the standard. FAS 157 has lengthy appendices to explain the amendments and modifications to previous pronouncements, as well as to give examples of applying its rules. The changes made to previous pronouncements should be reflected in the amended infobase. The CPA exam should be asking relatively straightforward research questions and should not require reading through the appendices of pronouncements. Therefore, it is wise to stay away from the appendices of FAS 157, as they are over 300 pages long. You do *not* have time to read appendices or potentially irrelevant material during the exam.

## FAS 158

FAS 158, issued in September 2006, is an important amendment to pension accounting. FAS 158 amends FAS 87, 88, 106, and 132(R). It applies to pension plans and other postretirement plans (OPEB). The most important aspect of FAS 158 is that companies must now recognize the funded status of a benefit plan. If a plan is overfunded, the overfunded amount is recorded as asset. If the plan is underfunded, the underfunded amount is recorded as a liability on the balance sheet. In addition, FAS 158 also amended the footnote disclosures for both pension plans and other postretirement plans. Because FAS 158 is an amendment to existing pronouncements, these changes should be incorporated into revised text in the amended version of the infobase. In other words, this is another research area where you may find your answer in two locations.

## FAS 159

FAS 159 is the new pronouncement covering the fair value option for financial assets and financial liabilities. FAS 159 is both a new pronouncement *and* contains and amendment of FAS 115. FAS 159 is an important pronouncement because it allows a company to elect the fair value option for certain financial assets and liabilities. Beware! FAS 159 contains scope limitations and includes a list of items that are not eligible for fair value reporting. The most important items in this list are pensions, other postretirement benefits, postemployment benefits, leases, and an investment in a subsidiary that must be consolidated.

FAS 159 has linkages with several other pronouncements. For example, prior to FAS 159, a company that owned more than 20% of the stock of another company and could exercise significant influence would use APB 18, the equity method of accounting. Recall that the equity method required a firm to include its share of the investee's income on the income statement, and required the investment account to be revalued by adding in its share of income and subtracting its share of dividends. Now, with FAS 159, a company can elect the fair value option for reporting an investment that would normally qualify for equity method treatment.

A second link can be seen with FAS 115. FAS 115 requires that trading securities are valued at fair value and any gain or loss is recorded in the income statement. That rule has not changed. However, FAS 115 also requires available-for-sale securities to be valued at fair value with any corresponding gain or loss being recognized in other comprehensive income (OCI). FAS 159 now allows the available-for-sale security to be revalued to fair value and the resulting gain or loss to be recognized in the income statement. FAS 115 requires that held-to-maturity securities are valued at amortized cost. FAS 159 now provides a fair value election that allows held-to-maturity securities to be valued at fair value with the resulting gain or loss included in the income statement.

Therefore, if you encounter a research problem on investment securities, read the question carefully. If the fair value option is elected, the rules of FAS 159 apply. If the fair value option is not elected, the rules of APB 28 or FAS 115 will apply depending upon the percentage of ownership.

Finally, there is a linkage between FAS 159 and FAS 157. FAS 157 provides the definition of fair value and the methods to calculate fair value. These rules generally apply to any item that is recorded at fair value. FAS 159 provides the rules for electing fair value treatment for specific items. Again, watch out for the scope limitations of FAS 159 because there are important exclusions.

## FAS 160

FAS 160, issued in December 2007, is the new standard for noncontrolling interests in financial statements.  FAS 160 amended ARB 51.  In other words, FAS 160 now has the rules for reporting minority interest in a subsidiary within the equity section of the balance sheet, but clearly labeled from the parent's equity.  In addition, FAS 160 requires that the amount of net income attributed to the noncontrolling interest is presented on the face of the consolidated income statement.

FAS 160 is effective for all years beginning on or after December 15, 2008.  Therefore, FAS 160 will be testable six months after that effective date, beginning with the July 2009 testing window.

## FAS 141(R)

FAS 141(R) revised FAS 141 and made significant changes in accounting for business combinations.  Similar to FAS 160, FAS 141(R) is effective for all years beginning on or after December 15, 2008.  Therefore, FAS 141(R) will be testable six months after the effective date, making it testable beginning with the July 2009 testing window.

### STAYING CURRENT

Candidates always ask, "Do I *really* need to know the newest standards?"  Let's discuss this from a strategic perspective.  The rule is that a new standard is testable 6 months after its effective date.  However, if early application is permitted, the standard is testable six months after its issue date.  On many of the newer standards, the FASB has permitted early application. Therefore, many new standards have been testable 6 months after the issue date.  Exceptions to this trend are the two most recent standards, FAS 160 and FAS 141(R).  Both FAS 160 and FAS 141(R) have delayed effective dates, and both FAS 160 and FAS 141(R) are testable six months after the effective date of December 15, 2008.

The next question is: When we are in a transition period, and both methods are permissible, which standard is testable?  *Both* are testable! Therefore, until the time period has elapsed, where all companies have converted to the new standard, both the old and the new standard could be tested.

Let's add more strategy to this issue. The AICPA uses pretest questions on the CPA exam.  In other words, the AICPA tests new questions for future versions of the exam.  So, if you were the AICPA and you were writing the exam, you would definitely want to pretest these new topics as soon as possible.

Here is *your* problem: when you see a question about a new standard on the exam, you have no idea if it is a *real* question that counts toward your grade or a *pretest* question.  And you certainly do not want to spend time worrying about which kind of question it is.  So my advice is—*learn the new standard*.  Do not leave passing the CPA exam up to chance.  There is no excuse for not knowing your content.  You are good, you are technical, and you are a professional.  So learn the new standard and prepare yourself well for the CPA exam.

Where does this leave us on the most recent standards?  Everything up to FAS 160 and FAS 141(R) are testable.  FAS 160 and FAS 141(R) should be testable as of July 2009.

In any event, as a professional entering your career, you are responsible for being current with the literature.  My advice: Stay current!

## QUICK REVIEW

Let's put this all together and make one big quick study list for the FASB Statements.  Exhibit 4.9 is our final study list for the FASB Statements.  Again, when you study this list, try chunking it into smaller groups of information, and think of the list as what's old, what's new, and what's in the middle.  That should help you locate the answer to a research question more quickly.

**Exhibit 4.9: FASB Statements Quick Study List**

| Number | Title of Standards |
|---|---|
| FAS 2 | Accounting for Research and Development Costs |
| FAS 5 | Accounting for Contingencies |
| FAS 6 | Classification of Short-Term Obligations Expected to Be Refinanced |
| FAS 13 | Accounting for Leases |
| FAS 15 | Accounting by Debtors and Creditors for Troubled Debt Restructurings |
| FAS 16 | Prior Period Adjustments |
| FAS 23 | Inception of the Lease |
| FAS 27 | Classification of Renewals or Extensions of Existing Sales-Type or Direct Financing Leases |
| FAS 28 | Accounting for Sales with Leasebacks |
| FAS 29 | Determining Contingent Rentals |
| FAS 34 | Capitalization of Interest Cost |
| FAS 43 | Accounting for Compensated Absences |
| FAS 45 | Accounting for Franchise Fee Revenue |
| FAS 47 | Disclosure of Long-Term Obligations |
| FAS 48 | Revenue Recognition When Right of Return Exists |
| FAS 49 | Accounting for Product Financing Arrangements |
| FAS 52 | Foreign Currency Translation |
| FAS 57 | Related-Party Disclosures |
| FAS 58 | Capitalization of Interest Cost in Financial Statements That Include Investments Accounted for by the Equity Method |
| FAS 66 | Accounting for Sales of Real Estate |

| Number | Title of Standards |
|---|---|
| FAS 67 | Accounting for Costs and Initial Rental Operations of Real Estate Projects |
| FAS 68 | Research and Development Arrangements |
| FAS 78 | Classification of Obligations That Are Callable by the Creditor |
| FAS 84 | Induced Conversions of Convertible Debt |
| FAS 86 | Accounting for the Costs of Computer Software to Be Sold, Leased, or Otherwise Marketed |
| FAS 87 | Employers' Accounting for Pensions |
| FAS 88 | Employers' Accounting for Settlements & Curtailments of Defined Benefit Pension Plans and for Termination Benefits |
| FAS 89 | Financial Reporting and Changing Prices |
| FAS 91 | Nonrefundable Fees & Costs Associated with Originating or Acquiring Loans and Initial Direct Costs of Leases |
| FAS 94 | Consolidation of All Majority-Owned Subsidiaries |
| FAS 95 | Statement of Cash Flows |
| FAS 98 | Accounting for Leases |
| FAS 106 | Employers' Accounting for Postretirement Benefits other than Pensions |
| FAS 107 | Disclosures about Fair Value of Financial Instruments |
| FAS 109 | Accounting for Income Taxes |
| FAS 112 | Employers' Accounting for Postemployment Benefits |
| FAS 114 | Accounting by Creditors for Impairment of a Loan |
| FAS 115 | Accounting for Certain Investments in Debt and Equity Securities |
| FAS 116 | Accounting for Contributions Received and Contributions Made |
| FAS 118 | Accounting by Creditors for Impairment of a Loan—Income Recognition and Disclosures |
| FAS 123(R) | Share-Based Payment |
| FAS 128 | Earnings per Share |
| FAS 129 | Disclosure of Information about Capital Structure |
| FAS 130 | Reporting Comprehensive Income |
| FAS 131 | Disclosures about Segments of an Enterprise and Related Information |
| FAS 132(R) | Employers' Disclosures about Pensions and Other Postretirement Benefits—an Amendment of FASB Statements No. 87, 88, and 106 |
| FAS 133 | Accounting for Derivative Instruments and Hedging Activities |
| FAS 138 | Accounting for Certain Derivative Instruments and Certain Hedging Activities—an Amendment of FASB Statement No. 133 |
| FAS 139 | Rescission of FASB Statement No. 53 and Amendments to FASB Statements No. 63, 89, and 121 |

| Number | Title of Standards |
|---|---|
| FAS 140 | Accounting for Transfers and Servicing of Financial Assets and Extinguishments of Liabilities |
| FAS 141 | Business Combinations |
| FAS 142 | Goodwill and Other Intangible Assets |
| FAS 143 | Accounting for Asset Retirement Obligations |
| FAS 144 | Accounting for the Impairment or Disposal of Long-Lived Assets |
| FAS 145 | Rescission of FASB Statements 4, 44, and 64, Amendment of FASB Statement No. 13, and Technical Corrections |
| FAS 146 | Accounting for Costs Associated with Exit or Disposal Activities |
| FAS 149 | Amendment of FASB Statement No. 133 on Derivative and Hedging Activities |
| FAS 150 | Accounting for Certain Financial Instruments with Characteristics of Both Liabilities and Equity |
| FAS 151 | Inventory Costs, an Amendment of ARB 43, Chapter 4 |
| FAS 152 | Accounting for Real Estate Time-Sharing Transactions |
| FAS 153 | Exchanges of Nonmonetary Assets—an Amendment of APB Opinion 29 |
| FAS 154 | Accounting Changes and Error Correction |
| FAS 155 | Accounting for Certain Hybrid Financial Instruments |
| FAS 156 | Accounting for Servicing of Financial Assets |
| FAS 157 | Fair Value Measurements |
| FAS 158 | Employers' Accounting for Defined Benefit Pension and Other Postretirement Plans |
| FAS 159 | The Fair Value Option for Financial Assets and Financial Liabilities |
| FAS 160 | Noncontrolling Interests in Consolidated Financial Statements—an Amendment or ARB 51 |
| FAS 141(R) | Business Combinations |

Now that we have a thorough understanding of the three types of standards (the ARBs, the APBs, and the FASB Statements), it is time to link these three types of standards and analyze the content more closely. Our next chapter will focus on content linkages.

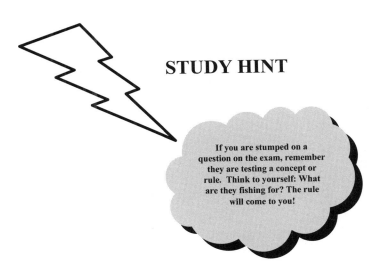

**STUDY HINT**

If you are stumped on a question on the exam, remember they are testing a concept or rule.  Think to yourself: What are they fishing for? The rule will come to you!

## TEST YOURSELF

**1.** Which standard contains the rules for capital leases?
- a. FAS 2.
- b. FAS 5.
- c. FAS 13.
- d. FAS 47.

**2.** Which of the following standards contains the rules for contingencies?
- a. FAS 5.
- b. FAS 27.
- c. FAS 48.
- d. FAS 109.

**3.** Which of the following topics has several FASB statements that address additional accounting issues related to that topic?
- a. Contingencies.
- b. Statement of cash flows.
- c. Leases.
- d. Foreign currency translations.

**4.** Which of the following standards contains the rules for pension accounting?
- a. FAS 45.
- b. FAS 87.
- c. FAS 109.
- d. FAS 115.

**5.** Which financial accounting topic had several pronouncements that the delayed effective date until a new pronouncement was written?
- a. Leases.
- b. Pensions.
- c. Income taxes.
- d. Earnings per share.

**6.** In which area of the accounting literature will you find the pronouncement for comprehensive income?
- a. Between FAS 10-20.
- b. Between FAS 70-90.
- c. Between FAS 123- 133.
- d. Between FAS 150-160.

**7.** Which of the following revised pronouncements changed the title of the pronouncement when it was revised?
- a. FAS 123(R).
- b. FAS 132(R).
- c. FAS 141(R).
- d. None of the above.

**8.** Which of the following standards defines trading securities, available-for-sale securities, and held-to-maturity securities?
- a. FAS 13.
- b. FAS 28.
- c. FAS 115.
- d. FAS 159.

**9.** Which accounting standard contains the accounting rules for accounting changes and error correction?
- a. FAS 141.
- b. FAS 145.
- c. FAS 151.
- d. FAS 154.

**10.** Which accounting standard outlines the requirements for related-party transactions?
- a. FAS 2.
- b. FAS 57.
- c. FAS 5.
- d. FAS 95.

## PRACTICE YOUR RESEARCH

Answer each of the following questions by finding the correct citation in the original pronouncements as amended.

1. At what amount should a lessee record a capital lease?

2. How does a firm determine whether a deferred tax liability is current or noncurrent?

3. What is the definition of fair value?

4. A company has current tax assets of $200 and noncurrent tax liabilities of $1,000. Can these two amounts be offset and presented as one item on the balance sheet?

5. A company may classify investments in securities in one of three ways. What are those classifications?

6. Can a gain contingency be recognized?

7. What is a bargain purchase option?

8. Jardin Corporation sells a franchise to Max Winthrop. When can the sale of the franchise be recognized by the franchisor?

9. Kendall has preferred stock that is convertible into shares of common stock. However, Kendall has calculated that the effect of conversion would be antidilutive. Should Kendall include the conversion of preferred stock in their calculation of diluted earnings per share?

10. How should a company report a change in accounting estimate?

# 5 FINANCIAL ACCOUNTING

## SELECTED TOPICS AND LINKAGES

Chapters 2 through 4 examined the organization and contents of the financial accounting literature. Recall that the Original Pronouncements as Amended are in chronological order. Therefore, if you study the standards in the order of the Original Pronouncements, it is easy to know what is old and what is new. Now it is time to look at some special topics and linkages within the standards. This will help you study certain topics in a more cohesive manner.

It is helpful to divide topical coverage into two groups. The first group of topics includes messy topics that have required several pronouncements or amendments to address all the various accounting issues. These are items such as leases, employment benefits, revenue recognition, investment securities, debt, and equity. This chapter will identify the linkages among the ARBs, the APBs, and the FASB statements. Identifying these linkages will help you understand the connections between the various standards and topics.

Then we'll look at some clear-cut pronouncements that are fairly self-contained. Those topics have relatively clear-cut pronouncements: earnings per share, segment reporting, statement of cash flows, business combinations, intangibles and goodwill, impairments, accounting changes, and share-based payments.

## LINKAGES BY TOPIC

### Leases

Leasing has historically been a messy issue. The basic issues for lease capitalization are found in FAS 13. In the definition area, you should realize that a capital lease is clearly defined if it meets *one* of the four criteria. However, the definition of operating lease is what I refer to as a "default" definition. In other words, if it does *not* meet one of the four criteria for a capital lease, then it is an operating lease. You need to be aware of this rule, so that you are not searching for a straightforward definition for the term operating lease.

The next important research issue for leases is the fact that FAS 13 has different rules for the lessor and the lessee. Definitions of terms, which apply to both the lessee and the lessor, are found near the beginning of the standard. In some instances, the definition is qualified, such as "from the standpoint of the lessee." Classification of leases is also handled in the same way with a different paragraph for the lessee and the lessor. FAS 13 then addresses the rules for lessee accounting first, beginning with paragraph 10. The rules for lessor accounting are later in the standard, beginning with paragraph 17. Remember that the rules for lessee and lessor are slightly different. Therefore, when researching lease issues, be *sure* to answer the question for the appropriate individual, either the lessee or the lessor.

Another issue regarding leases is that the problem may have clearly identified that the transaction is classified as a capital lease. However, there may be other leasing issues that must be resolved. For example, what if the lease payments are not the same each year (uneven payments)? What if there is a contingent rental agreement? What if the lease term is extended? What if the lease is terminated early? What if the lessee makes leasehold improvements? What happens if a company sells something and then leases it back? How does one account for loan origination fees? What happens if part of the company is being disposed of by sale and leases must be cancelled? What if, what if, what if?

FASB, of course, was required to address these issues after FAS 13 was issued. Several later pronouncements resolve or clarify these issues that were not addressed by FAS 13. Exhibit 5.1 outlines the group of pronouncements that clarify leasing issues. Keep in mind, everything is post-FAS 13, so nothing on leases is found in the earlier ARB and APB literature.

**Exhibit 5.1: Linkages in the Standards: Leases**

| Number | Topic | Issues/Rules |
|--------|-------|--------------|
| FAS 13 | Leases | Basic rules for capital and operator leases for lessee and lessor |
| FAS 23 | Inception of Lease | Replaces or amends several paragraphs in FAS 13. Date of lease is lease agreement or commitment date, if earlier. |
| FAS 27 | Renewals or Extensions | Issue is how is lease classified (direct financing or sales-type lease) if lease is renewed. |
| FAS 28 | Sales Leaseback | Supersedes certain paragraphs in FAS 13. Changed in Original Pronouncements as Amended and cross-referenced. |
| FAS 29 | Contingent Rentals | Additions and amendments to FAS 13. Contingent rentals are excluded from minimum lease payment |
| FAS 91 | Loan Origination Fees | Lessors account for initial direct costs as part of the investment in a direct financing lease. |
| FAS 98 | Sales Leaseback for Real Estate | This is for real estate sales-leasebacks. Regular sales-leasebacks is FAS 28. |

| Number | Topic | Issues/ Rules |
|--------|-------|---------------|
| FAS 145 | Rescission, Amendments and Technical Corrections to Various Standards | If capital lease is modified and results in classification of operating lease, the rules of sales-leasebacks in FAS 28 and FAS 98 apply. |
| FAS 146 | Exit or Disposal Activities | Rules for terminating an operating lease |

Again, don't try to memorize this list.  It is sufficient to be aware of which items are the exceptions to the lease rules found in FAS 13 and are located in a different standard.  Remember, you do not want to spend 20 minutes trying to find something in FAS 13 when it isn't there!

Also, note that many of the items in Exhibit 5-1 are amendments to FAS 13.  In particular, FAS 23, 27, 28, 29, and 145 are amendments to FAS 13.  Therefore, you may find your answer in two different places in the infobase—both in FAS 13 as amended and in the later standard.  Don't let this redundancy confuse you.

FAS 145 deserves special attention because this standard does not have a descriptive title.  It is a catchall pronouncement for technical corrections and amendment that addresses many issues.  The lease issue is near the end and is somewhat difficult to find.  However, because FAS 145 is an amendment to FAS 13, the answer may be found in two places: both in FAS 13 and FAS 145.  Knowing these redundancies exist in the infobase will help reduce any confusion when conducting research on the exam.

Make sure you are familiar with the titles of these exception items.  Familiarity with exceptions to the basic rules will cue you as to when it is necessary to use a keyword search or to look for another standard for your answer.  And be sure you are aware of the two newest changes in FAS 145 and 146 that deal with changing a capital lease to an operating lease or terminating on operating lease.  If you are aware of these changes, you can easily find these rules.

**Revenue Recognition**

Our next challenging set of pronouncements is the set of pronouncements that addresses revenue recognition issues.  First, the basic definition of revenue, revenue recognition, realized, recognized, etc. are in the FASB Concept Statements.  The Concept Statements are the lowest level of authority in GAAP.

There is no one comprehensive standard on revenue recognition.  A brief discussion of determination of income is found in ARB 43.  However, in most cases, you need to look at the *type* of revenue, and find the standard for that particular item.  The common types of revenue that you will find are installment revenue, franchising revenue, leasing revenue, real estate revenue, product financing arrangements, software revenue, and sales with right of return.  Let's list these in the order in which they were issued, so you have a good historical picture in your mind.  Exhibit 5.2 outlines the various pronouncements for revenue recognition.

**Exhibit 5.2: Linkages in the Standards: Revenue Recognition Issues**

| Number | Topic | Comments/Rules/Keywords |
|---|---|---|
| ARB 43 | Income Determination | Chapter 4 and Chapter 7 mention determination of income and proper matching of expenses |
| ARB 45 | Long-Term Construction-Type Contracts | Percentage-of-completion and completed-contract method |
| APB 10 | Installment method | Reaffirms that revenue should be accounted for at the time transaction is completed. |
| APB 29 | Nonmonetary Exchanges | If transaction has economic substance, recognize gain |
| FAS 13 | Leases | Lessor recognizes interest income in direct financing lease; lessor recognizes sale and cost of goods sold in sales-type lease, but also recognizes interest revenue over life of lease |
| FAS 45 | Franchising | Recognize revenue when all material service or conditions relating to the sale have been substantially performed by franchisor. |
| FAS 48 | Sales with Right of Return | Recognize revenue only if all six conditions are met, (i.e., price fixed or determinable at date of sale, buyer has obligation to pay, etc).  See the list of six rules in this standard! |
| FAS 49 | Product Financing Arrangements | If seller sells goods and agrees to repurchase the inventory, then account for as a borrowing rather than sale. |
| FAS 66 | Real Estate | When to recognize revenue for construction or development projects. When to use percentage-of-completion or installment method |
| FAS 140 | Transfers and Servicing of Financial Assets | Sale of receivables |

Real estate is another area that may have special rules for revenue recognition.  Since real estate is more in the special interest area, we have deleted some of the real estate standards from our list.  However, if you do encounter a question, be aware that these rules are scattered throughout the pronouncements in FAS 66, 67, 98, and 152.

## Liabilities

Another hot topic is liabilities. The accounting rules for liabilities focus on the type of liability (payables, warranties, contingencies, long-term debt, etc.), the valuation of the liability, the classification of the liability (current or noncurrent), financial statement disclosures, and footnote disclosures. Then you have all of the "what if" issues. What if they issued convertible debt? What if they issued debts with warrants? What if they redeem the debt early? What if the debtor can't pay the loan? What if?

Again, before you research, you need to narrow the issue so you know where to look. The detailed rules for various issues with debt are *all over* the standards. Awareness of the various issues and knowing the correct vocabulary is helpful in finding these issues.

The old term for troubled debt restructuring is now referred to as loan impairment. Of course, troubled debt restructuring is the term for the debtor—this is the company who can't pay the debt who is restructuring. The rules for debtor are found in FAS 15. The other side of the loan is the creditor. The rules for the creditor have been changed and are now called loan impairment. The rules for the creditor are found in FAS 114.

Exhibit 5.3 is a listing of the most common issues with debt. I've tried to identify some of the issues, rules, or keywords to help you search for these topics. I've kept these in chronological order of the standards so you can get a feeling for what is old material and what is newer material.

**Exhibit 5.3: Linkages in the Standards: Liabilities**

| Number | Topic | Issues/Rules/Keywords |
|---|---|---|
| ARB 43 | Classification of Liabilities | When to classify liability as current or noncurrent. See Ch 3A, par. 7 |
| APB 12 | Premiums/Discounts | How to amortize—(calculation for amortization.) |
| APB 14 | Convertible Debt and Debt with stock warrants | Allocate proceeds to detachable warrants and account for as paid-in capital based on relative fair values of securities |
| APB 21 | Notes Payable | How to value notes, effective interest, F/S presentation of discounts and premiums |
| APB 26 | Early Extinguishment of Debt | Recognize difference between cash acquisition price and net carrying amount of debt as gain or loss |
| FAS 5 | Contingencies | Accounting disclosure depends if it is probable, possible, or remote. |
| FAS 6 | Classification of Liability Expected to Be Refinanced | Amends ARB 43, Ch 3A. Classify as long-term is intent to refinance the obligation on a long-term basis *and* have the ability to consummate the refinancing |

| Number | Topic | Issues/Rules/Keywords |
|---|---|---|
| FAS 15 | Troubled Debt Restructuring | Rules for debtor |
| FAS 43 | Compensated Absences | Recognize liability for employee accrued benefits |
| FAS 47 | Disclosure of Long-term Obligations | Disclosure of future payments on long-term borrowings and redeemable stock. Maturities and sinking fund requirements for each of next five years. |
| FAS 84 | Induced Conversions of Convertible Debt | Sweeteners to induce conversions of debt are an expense |
| FAS 91 | Loan Origination Fees | Defer and recognize over life of loan as adjustment to yield |
| FAS 114 | Creditors of Impaired Loans | Rules for creditors for impaired loans |

The most important point to remember about debt is that the rules are scattered among the pronouncements. If you encounter a question on the exam and you cannot remember where the topic is located, try using keywords. If you experience difficulty with keyword searches, try using the topical index or the current text. You may find some citations or links there that will help you gain speed on finding the answer. Remember, time is your enemy on the research part of the CPA exam, so you may want to review this area more thoroughly to become more familiar with the standards.

**Stockholders' Equity**

Some of the stockholders' equity material is old. Specifically, the older areas include issuing stock, treasury stock transactions, stock dividends, stock split-ups, and property dividends. This is also an area where you will see more antiquated vocabulary. Therefore, you may have difficulty finding issues with keyword searches if your vocabulary is not precise.

In earlier days, it was called capital surplus (not additional paid-in capital, paid-in capital in excess of par, or paid-in capital). It was also called profit or loss; now it's net income or net loss. We talked of stock split-ups, not stock splits.

And here is my personal favorite: When we talk about dividends, we think of cash dividends, small stock dividends, large stock dividends, and property dividends. In the standards, ARB 43, Ch 7B, par. 10 explains that "where issuances are so small in comparison with the shares previously outstanding" the company should "account for the transaction by transferring from earned surplus to the category of permanent capitalization an amount equal to the fair value of the additional shares issued." In English? Small dividends are recorded at fair value. We debit retained earnings for fair value of the stock issued and credit the common stock and additional paid-in capital account. Notice that the standard does not state the rule so succinctly or with today's vocabulary!

Even more fascinating is the next paragraph. ARB 43, Ch 7B, par. 11 is even more convoluted when describing how to account for a "large" stock dividend. Notice the paragraph never says the word *large*, it states it as "so great." The rule further states that it is a split-up effected in the form of a dividend. And don't forget the 20-25% rule for determining what is a large and what is a small dividend. That's right behind the stock dividend material in paragraph 13. I'd recommend looking at this just for fun. It is almost impossible to find in a keyword search. However, once you see where it is, you'll never forget it!

Another entertaining rule to find is the rule for property dividends. Of course, we know the rule is that property dividends are recorded at fair value. But if you are using those keywords, you probably won't find your answer. Property dividends are discussed in APB 29 under nonmonetary transactions. The paragraph that explains the rule (APB 29, par. 5) calls it a "nonreciprocal transfer with owners" and a "nonmonetary distribution to stockholders as dividends." Then, later, in APB 29, par. 18, it explains that the transfer is recorded at fair value. This valuation rule is in the *Opinion* paragraph.

Again, the citation is somewhat cryptic; it is listed as a nonreciprocal transfer to owners—old vocabulary. The paragraph never uses the words "property dividend." That's some very fancy terminology for trying to find the rule that property dividends are valued at fair value. This rule is almost impossible to find with a keyword search.

If you do encounter a research question with an issue for stockholders' equity, try to remember the vocabulary here. Also, remember which are the older issues and which are the newer issues. The older pronouncements focus on issuing stock, paying dividends, recording stock warrants, repurchasing treasury stock, and reorganizations. The more recent pronouncements address some problem areas with stockholders' equity, such as the newer EPS rules, hybrid securities, and share-based payments. Let's look at a list that outlines the stockholders' equity topics.

Exhibit 5.4 outlines the linkages for various stockholders' equity issues. Again, focus on older topics and newer topics, and it will be easier to remember where certain rules are located.

**Exhibit 5.4: Linkages in the Standards: Stockholders' Equity**

| Number | Topic | Issues/Rules/Keywords |
|---|---|---|
| ARB 43 | Treasury Stock | Ch 1B, par. 7—No profit or loss on treasury stock. Cannot show treasury stock as an asset on balance sheet. Linked to APB 6 for journal entries for treasury stock. |
| ARB 43 | Stock Dividends and Stock Splits | Ch 7B, par. 10, 11 and 13. Rules and valuation of stock dividends. |
| APB 6 | Treasury Stock | Amendment to ARB 43—journal entries for retirement of treasury stock and holding treasury stock |
| APB 14 | Warrants | Allocate proceeds to detachable warrants and account for as paid-in capital based on relative fair values of securities |
| APB 29 | Property Dividends | Nonreciprocal transfers to owners are valued at fair value of the asset. |
| FAS 123(R) | Share Based Payments | Supersedes everything on stock options. Is more comprehensive because shares can be paid to employee or nonemployee |
| FAS 128 | Earnings Per Share | Comprehensive rules for basic and diluted EPS |
| FAS 129 | Disclosures for Capital Structure | Disclosures on the face of financial statements and in footnotes of number of shares, rights and privileges of securities outstanding |
| FAS 130 | Reporting Comprehensive Income | Rules for comprehensive income and other comprehensive income |
| FAS 150 | Mandatorily Redeemable Stock | Mandatory redeemable preferred stock is classified as a liability |

## Employee Benefits

There are many benefits that employers can bestow upon their employees. Vacation pay, sick days, pension benefits, other postretirement benefits such as health insurance or life insurance, and postemployment benefits when employee leaves the firm for other reasons such as resignation or termination. Each of these topics is in a separate pronouncement.

FAS 43 addresses the issues of vacation pay and sick pay for employees. FAS 43 is titled *Compensated Absences*. The big issue is that as an employee earns vacation pay and sick pay, the employer should accrue a liability for these days.

FAS 87 is the *big* pronouncement on pensions. FAS 106 is the big pronouncement on other postretirement benefits (OPEB). When these two pronouncements were first promulgated, the additional disclosures in the notes to financial statements were listed near the end of each standard.  However, a few years later, those disclosures were not considered sufficient.  Therefore, in 1998, the FASB issued a new standard, FAS 132, requiring certain footnote disclosures for both pensions and OPEB.  Later, this new set of disclosures was also changed, and yet a *newer* standard was issued outlining another set of disclosures.  The pronouncement that now contains the current set of required financial statements disclosures is in FAS 132(R), issued in 2004.  FAS 132(R) supersedes the original FAS 132 and amends FAS 87 and 106.  Therefore, you might find the footnote disclosures in two places: in each of the amended statements or in FAS 132(R).

Another standard, FAS 112, issued in 1992, addressed postemployment benefits.  These are benefits for former or inactive employees.  The benefits include payments for severance benefits, disability benefits, job training, health insurance, and life insurance.  FAS 112 amends FAS 5 and FAS 43, so you might find the rules cross-referenced in both places.

An important issue in research on employee benefits is to remember the correct spelling in keyword searches.  For example, is postemployment one word, two words, or hyphenated?  You may see different results if you type in *post employment*, *post-employment*, or *postemployment*.  In the standards, *postretirement* and *postemployment* are one word without a hyphen.  Make a mental note of that; it may save you valuable time on the exam.

### Investments

The accounting rules for investments are different depending on the type of investment, the percentage of ownership, and whether an election is made to use the fair value option.  The list of accounting standards for investments and a brief outline of key issues are shown in Exhibit 5.5.

**Exhibit 5.5: Linkages in the Standards: Investments**

| Number | Topic | Issues/Rules/Keywords |
|--------|-------|------------------------|
| ARB 51 | Business Combinations | Intercompany transactions and minority interest rules |
| APB 18 | Equity Method | Significant influence.  Greater than 20-25% ownership. |
| FAS 115 | Trading, AFS, and HTM Securities | Fair value method for securities |
| FAS 141 | Business Combinations | Purchase method and accounting at time of acquisition.  Revised by FAS 141(R) effective for fiscal years beginning after December 15, 2008. |
| FAS 159 | Fair Value Option | Elect fair value option |
| FAS 160 | Minority Interests in Subsidiary | Noncontrolling interests in consolidated financial statements |

FAS 159, issued in February 2007, allows a company to elect the fair value option for recording financial assets and financial liabilities.  Prior to

FAS 159, a researcher examined the percentage of ownership of the investee. If the company owned less than 20% and had no significant influence, the rules of FAS 115 applied If the company owned between 20% and 50% and could exercise significant influence, the rules of APB 18, equity method, applied. If a company owned more than 50% and controlled the company, then consolidated statements were prepared, and the rules of FAS 141 and ARB 51 applied.

If FAS 115 applied, the researcher was required to make another distinction as to the classification of the investment: trading securities, available-for-sale securities, or held-to-maturity securities. Although trading and available-for-sale securities are both marked to fair value at year-end, the recognition of the gain or loss was handled differently. Therefore, in a research problem, it is important to read the problem carefully to distinguish how the investment was classified.

FAS 159 has significantly changed accounting for investments. If the fair value method is elected, a company no longer must use the rules of APB 18 or FAS 115. FAS 159 allows the securities to be valued to fair value at the reporting date, with the resulting gain or loss included in income. Remember, though, that this is an *election*, so be sure to read the problem carefully to determine if the fair value option is elected. If the fair value option is not elected, then the rules of APB 18 or FAS 115, depending on the percentage of ownership, will apply.

Another issue to understand with FAS 159 is that FAS 159 is very specific in its scope. The fair value option does *not* apply to an investment that is required to consolidate, a variable-interest entity that is required to consolidate, pensions, other postretirement benefits, postemployment benefits, leases as defined in FAS 13, or financial instruments that are a component of shareholders' equity. However, it *does* apply to certain insurance contracts and warranties that can be settled by paying a third party to provide the services.

## Business Combinations

The last issue in investments that merits discussion is the recent change in FAS 141 on business combinations. FAS 141(R), issued in December 2007, significantly changed the accounting for business combinations. In addition, FAS 160, also issued in December 2007, changed the reporting for minority interests. Both FAS 141(R) and FAS 160 are effective for fiscal years beginning after December 15, 2008. Therefore, it appears FAS 141(R) and FAS 160 should become testable in the July 2009 testing window.

ARB 51, FAS 94, and FAS 141 are the authoritative pronouncements for business combinations until FAS 141(R) and FAS 160 are effective. Recall that ARB 51 is the old consolidations standard. Most of ARB 51 is superseded by FAS 141. The contents of ARB 51 that remain in effect today are the rules for intercompany transactions and minority interest. FAS 94 requires consolidation of all majority-owned subsidiaries unless control is temporary or does not rest with the majority owner. FAS 141 eliminated the pooling method and requires business combinations to be accounted for by the purchase method.

An important point to make is that FAS 141 addresses newly identified assets and goodwill *at the date* of acquisition. FAS 141 is the standard that provides the valuation rule for initially valuing and recording goodwill. After the date of acquisition, FAS 142 steps in and identifies the rules for accounting for goodwill and intangibles. This is an important distinction in research. If you encounter a research question that involves the amortization or impairment of goodwill, those answers are found in FAS 142.

### Not for Profit

So far, we have not discussed research in the not-for-profit (NFP) area. If you should receive a research question in this area, there are three FASB standards that specifically address not-for- profit issues. FAS 93, FAS 117, and FAS 124. Remember, we deleted these from our quick study list, so you need to be aware of these standards. Exhibit 5.6 is a listing of the not-for-profit standards. Keep in mind, we casually refer to these organizations as nonprofit organizations, but in the literature, the keyword is "not-for-profit."

**Exhibit 5.6: Linkages in the Standards: Not-for-Profit Organizations**

| FAS 93 | Recognition of Depreciation by Not-for-Profit Organizations |
|---|---|
| FAS 117 | Financial Statements of Not-for-Profit Organizations |
| FAS 124 | Accounting for Certain Investments Held by Not-for-Profit Organizations |

## STAND-ALONE PRONOUNCEMENTS

As we discussed in Chapter 4, the FASB statements can be viewed as falling into one of three categories:

- Creates a new set of rules for a specific topic or issue
- Amends one pronouncement
- Amends several pronouncements

This is an important distinction for studying the pronouncements. Stand-alone pronouncements are easier to remember. They have clear titles that are descriptive of their contents. When conducting research, these pronouncements are easy to find using a drop-down menu of the pronouncement number and titles. In addition, if you know the stand-alone pronouncement number, you can easily perform a search within for the specific issue being researched.

A pronouncement that amends only one pronouncement is also easy to locate because the nature of the amendment is usually in the title of the standard. Since the CPA exam should be using an amended version of the infobase, it is important to understand that the answer can be found in two places. Knowing this will save valuable time on the exam by eliminating the confusion with these redundancies.

The third type of standard, the "catchall" type of pronouncement that amends several standards, is more difficult to locate. For example, FAS 145 supersedes and amends a variety of rules for unrelated topics in several previous pronouncements. These catchall standards are more difficult to remember, and the titles are not always clear. If you are using the Original Pronouncements on the FARS CD, the amendments are adequately cross-referenced in the Original Pronouncements and marked with a red jump link to take you to the new rule. If you are using the Original Pronouncements as Amended on the FARS CD, these amendments have been added to the older pronouncements by editing the previous pronouncements. On the CPA exam, the version of the infobase should be the Original Pronouncements as Amended, so the new material should be included in the revised version of the standard. However, remember that if you conduct a keyword search, your results may indicate the answer is in two places.

Let's quickly review a few of the most important stand-alone pronouncements.

### FAS 5—*Accounting for Contingencies*

FAS 5 is an important standard because it defines the term contingency and outlines the conditions when an estimated loss must be accrued and charged to income. To find this easily in the infobase with a keyword search, type in the words "probable reasonably possible remote" and the search engine should take you directly to FAS 5. Using these more precise keywords will eliminate extraneous material that you would encounter in the results list if you only used the keywords *contingency* or *contingencies*.

### FAS 34—*Capitalization of Interest Cost*

FAS 34, issued in 1979, is a relatively old pronouncement. Although it may have had a few amendments by later pronouncements, FAS 34 contains the basic rules for capitalizing interest cost as a part of the historical cost of acquiring certain assets. Notice the standard uses the words *interest cost* and not the term *interest expense*.

### FAS 52—*Foreign Currency Translation*

FAS 52 contains the rules for foreign currency translation. FAS 52 defines functional currency, the exchange rate(s) to be used, and financial statement disclosures related to foreign currency translations. FAS 52 also defines foreign currency transactions and the rules for recognizing a gain or loss on a foreign currency transaction. However, FAS 133 amended some paragraphs relating to forward contracts and hedging.

### FAS 87—*Employers' Accounting for Pensions*

FAS 87 is another stand-alone pronouncement, but it has been amended by several other pronouncements. The most recent amendment is FAS 158, that requires the overfunded or underfunded status of the plan be disclosed in the balance sheet. These changes should be incorporated into the amended version of the infobase on the CPA exam. Therefore, you can expect to find the rules on pensions to be in FAS 87. However, footnote disclosures were amended by FAS 132(R). Because FAS 132(R) amended certain paragraphs and replaced other paragraphs in FAS 87, you may find the footnote disclosures for pensions in two different locations. For research purposes on the CPA exam, you should be able to rely on the amended version of FAS 87 for most of your research needs on pensions.

### FAS 95—*Statement of Cash Flows*

FAS 95 is an exceptional stand-alone pronouncement that has withstood the test of time. It is well-written, easy to read, and clear. Definitions are in the front of the standard. Content, form of the statement, and reconciliation issues are near the end. Don't forget that there are amendments made by FAS 115 for trading securities, available-for-sale securities, and held-to-maturity securities. There are also amendments made to FAS 115 by FAS 159, but these amendments should be incorporated into the revised text of the standards. Watch out for spelling and the potential need to use hyphens in keyword searches.

### FAS 115—*Certain Investments in Debt and Equity Securities*

Again, this is another well-written standard. There are only 25 paragraphs to this statement. The general rules are in the front, classification issues for changing a security from one category to another are more toward the end of the standard, and footnote disclosures are near the end of the standard. However, be sure to read the research question carefully. If the research question indicates that the fair value option is elected, FAS 115 rules no longer apply, and the security is valued using the rules in FAS 159.

### FAS 123(R)—*Share-Based Payment*

FAS 123(R), entitled *Share-Based Payment*, revises the old FAS 123, *Accounting for Stock-Based Compensation,* and supersedes APB 25, *Accounting for Stock Issued to Employees.* The organization of FAS 123(R) is very specific. The scope is always in the front of a pronouncement. Recognition rules are at the beginning of the standard. However, specific rules vary depending on whether the payment is to employees, nonemployees, related parties and other economic interest holders, or to employee share purchase plans. The second important research issue is whether the payment is classified as liability or equity. This standard has 85 paragraphs with some lengthy transition rules located at the end of the standard. If you encounter a research case on share-based payments, be sure to read the problem carefully to determine the identity of the party receiving the payment and whether the payment is described as equity or a liability.

### FAS 128—*Earnings Per Share*

FAS 128 is the standard on earnings per share. FAS 128 is relatively brief and easy to read. Basic earnings per share rules are near the beginning of the standard. Diluted earnings per share rules begin with paragraph 11. Presentation rules for EPS and special presentation rules for effects of discontinued operations and extraordinary items are near the end of the standard, but before the footnote disclosures. Although FAS 128 has undergone minor amendments with some of the newer standards such as FAS 154, any of these changes should be reflected in the amended version of the standard. Therefore, FAS 128 should be the primary place a researcher would search to answer a question regarding earnings per share.

### FAS 130—*Reporting Comprehensive Income*

FAS 130 is entitled *Reporting Comprehensive Income.* This title is interesting because accountants normally refer to items as part of other comprehensive income or accumulated other comprehensive income. Therefore, although we may refer to it as OCI or AOCI in our everyday language, when researching you may need to refrain from using the extra words to find the appropriate paragraphs for a particular research question.

### FAS 133—*Accounting for Derivative Instruments and Hedging Activities*

FAS 133. What can I say about derivatives that could possibly make this topic more lovable? Nothing. The topic is derivatives. Paragraphs have been amended and replaced by FAS 137, 138, 140, 149, 150, and 155. Any changes should be reflected in the amended version of the infobase. This has traditionally been a messy topic. Hopefully, a research question would be limited to a simple question involving a definition or the requirement that the instrument is measured at fair value.

### FAS 140—*Accounting for Transfers and Servicing of Financial Assets and Extinguishment of Liabilities*

FAS 140 replaced FAS 125. Although several later pronouncements such as FAS 153, 156, and 157 amended and changed FAS 140, the changes should be included in the revised version of the standard. Therefore, you should be able to rely on FAS 140 for any research question on transfers and servicing of financial assets.

## FAS 141—*Business Combinations*

FAS 141 was the comprehensive stand-alone pronouncement regarding business combinations until December 2007, when the Financial Accounting Standards Board issued FAS 141(R). However, FAS 141(R) has a delayed effective date and is effective for all fiscal years beginning after December 15, 2008. Therefore, FAS 141(R) should not be testable until six months after the effective date, which would be the July 2009 testing window. Although current accounting courses will likely teach the new standard, CPA candidates should rely on the original FAS 141 for research purposes until the effective date.

## FAS 142—*Goodwill and Other Intangibles*

As discussed earlier in this chapter, FAS 142 outlines the rules for goodwill *after* the acquisition date. FAS 142 also redefines the term goodwill. In layman's terms goodwill is considered an intangible. However, for purposes of FAS 142, goodwill is not considered an intangible for the purpose of that particular statement. In other words, goodwill is classified as goodwill and has its own rules. FAS 142 further distinguishes intangibles as two different types: intangibles subject to amortization and intangibles not subject to amortization. This distinction is based on intangibles with definite lives and intangibles with indefinite lives. Notice here that the word is *indefinite*, not infinite. Therefore, there are three sets of rules in FAS 142: rules for intangibles with finite lives, rules for intangibles with indefinite lives, and rules for goodwill.

FAS 142 also deals with the impairment of intangible assets and the tests for impairment on those intangibles. Again, FAS 142 addresses impairment of goodwill separately. If you encounter a research question on any of these topics, you should be able to use the drop-down menus to look for the correct document title to guide you to the answer.

## FAS 144—*Impairment or Disposal of Long-Lived Assets*

FAS 144 outlines the rules for impairment or disposal of long-lived assets. Again, the interesting part about this standard is that it is also divided into four distinct parts. The rules can be found grouped by assets to be held and used, assets to be disposed of by other than sale, assets to be disposed of by sale, and discontinued operations. Notice that discontinued operations is near the end of this statement. If you have a research question on impairment or disposals, read the question carefully so you identify the type of asset impaired (i.e., held and used, or held for sale).

### FAS 154—*Accounting Changes*

FAS 154 is a relatively new statement that is well-organized and easy to follow. The definitions are clearly stated at the beginning of the pronouncement. Again, it groups the accounting rules into four topics: change in principle, change in estimate, change in reporting entity, and correction of error. The rules and the footnote disclosures for each type of change are found within each topic.

## DEVELOPING A RESEARCH STRATEGY

Now that you are very familiar with the authoritative literature, it is important to develop a research strategy. First, beware of amendments! Sometimes the accounting rules will be found in two places because you are using the Original Pronouncements as Amended. Other topic areas have a standard that is complete and "stands alone." As you study, try to make a mental note of which of the standards are complete and which are stand-alone. Knowing what is stand-alone material will build your confidence and save time looking for any other material.

Remember, *order* is important. Both the order of the standards, and the order of the content within the standard are important. You need to know whether you should be looking in the ARBs, APBs, or the FASB Statements. Then, you need to think whether you should be looking for your answer in the beginning, middle, or end of the standard.

We'll discuss more on research strategy in Chapter 9, Getting Ready for the Exam.

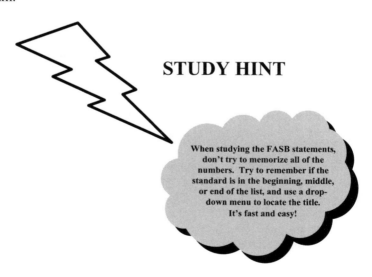

**STUDY HINT**

When studying the FASB statements, don't try to memorize all of the numbers. Try to remember if the standard is in the beginning, middle, or end of the list, and use a drop-down menu to locate the title. It's fast and easy!

## TEST YOURSELF

**1.** Which standard outlines the rules for accounting changes?
    a.  FAS 5.
    b.  FAS 128.
    c.  FAS 141.
    d.  FAS 154.

**2.** Which of the following standards contains the rules for discontinued operations?
    a.  FAS 13.
    b.  FAS 95.
    c.  FAS 144.
    d.  FAS 160.

**3.** A company holds investments securities as an asset and classifies them as a held-to-maturity investment. The company elects the fair value option for reporting the securities. Which of the following standards applies?
    a.  APB 28.
    b.  FAS 115.
    c.  FAS 141.
    d.  FAS 159.

**4.** Where would you most likely find the rules for revenue recognition for a sale that is made using the installment method of payment?
    a.  APB 10.
    b.  FAS 66.
    c.  FAS 45.
    d.  FAS 140.

**5.** Where will you find the accounting rules that explain the accounting treatment for compensated absences to employees?
    a.  ARB 43.
    b.  FAS 43.
    c.  FAS 87.
    d.  FAS 140.

**6.** The rules for accounting for a property dividend are included in which area of the infobase?
    a.  ARB 43 in the stockholders' equity area.
    b.  APB 6 with the opinions on treasury stock.
    c.  FAS 123 with share-based payments.
    d.  APB 29 with nonmonetary exchanges.

**7.** For purposes of FAS 142, is goodwill an intangible asset?
    a.  Yes.
    b.  No.

**8.** Where are the rules for earnings per share located in the infobase?
    a.  FAS 115.
    b.  ARB 43.
    c.  FAS 128.
    d.  APB 21.

**9.** Which standard identifies the disclosure of long-term obligations on the financial statements?
    a.  ARB 43.
    b.  FAS 47.
    c.  FAS 91.
    d.  FAS 144.

**10.** Which standard outlines the conditions for probable, reasonably possible, and remote with regard to contingencies?
    a.  ARB 43.
    b.  APB 21.
    c.  FAS 5.
    d.  FAS 84.

## PRACTICE YOUR RESEARCH SKILLS

1. What are the five components of pension cost in a defined benefit pension plan?

2. For purposes of foreign currency translations, what is the definition of an entity's functional currency?

3. What are the conditions that must be met for revenue recognition purposes if a seller gives the buyer a right of return?

4. Can goodwill be amortized?

5. What is considered the date of the inception of a capital lease?

6. A company chooses to use the percentage-of-completion method for recognizing revenue on construction projects. How does the company determine how much income to recognize the first year?

7. Lorax Corporation pays a trucking company $300 to deliver items to its warehouse. These items will be sold to customers. How should Lorax classify the $300 paid to the trucking company?

8. On October 1, 2008, Ardent Corporation signed a contract to purchase 1,000 pieces of inventory from Company X for $100,000. The contract is irrevocable. In December 2008, Ardent learns that the inventory is worth only $85,000 and will be delivered in February 2009. Should Ardent recognize a loss in the 2008 income statement?

9. Ronan uses the equity method of accounting for its 25% interest in Rex Corporation. How should Ronan record its share of income from Rex?

10. Jamison received a note receivable in exchange for cash. At what amount should the note receivable be recorded in the balance sheet?

# 6 AUDITING AND ATTESTATION RESEARCH

The Auditing and Attestation (AUD) section of the CPA exam has historically been challenging for CPA candidates. However, the research component on AUD has been reported by some candidates to be easier than the research components in FAR or REG. Candidates may find AUD research easier for several reasons. First, the Professional Standards have very descriptive titles. Second, the standards have been codified into one cohesive set of pronouncements. Therefore, it may be easier to find the literature because the codified standards are current, nicely labeled, and located in one place. One of the challenges you will face is making *sure* you are in the correct part of the infobase for the type of engagement you are researching.

## AUDITING STANDARD SETTING BODIES

Prior to the Sarbanes-Oxley Act of 2002, the auditing standards were set by the Auditing Standards Board (ASB), a committee of the AICPA. Although the ASB is still in existence, the auditing standards of the ASB apply to all **nonpublic** traded entities. The Sarbanes-Oxley Act of 2002 gave the authority for standard setting in auditing for **public** companies to the Public Company Accounting Oversight Board (PCAOB).

Now here's the interesting part. The PCAOB adopted the first ten Generally Accepted Auditing Standards (GAAS). The PCAOB also adopted certain preexisting standards of the ASB as interim standards. These interim standards are to be used on a transitional basis. In instances where the PCAOB-generated standard is different from the ASB standard, the PCAOB standard applies.

As of January 2008, the PCAOB has issued five auditing standards with the abbreviation AS. Note that the PCAOB standards are not effective until approved by the SEC. Exhibit 6.1 is a list of the first four auditing standards issued by the PCAOB that are in effect as of January 2008.

Theoretically, candidates are responsible for knowing all appropriate standards for the CPA exam. It is possible, therefore, that both sets of standards are on the CPA exam. For publicly traded companies, the PCAOB standards apply. For nonpublic companies, the ASB standards apply. In most instances, the AICPA has attempted to include the newer PCAOB standards in their infobase. You will find these additions in each of the appropriate standards.

**Exhibit 6.1:  PCAOB Standards as of January 2008**

| Number | Title |
|---|---|
| AS 1 | References in Auditors' Report to the Standards of the PCAOB |
| AS 2 | An Audit of Internal Control over Financial Reporting Performed in Conjunction with an Audit of Financial Statements |
| AS 3 | Audit Documentation |
| AS 4 | Reporting on Whether a Previously Reported Material Weakness Continues to Exist (effective February 6, 2006) |
| AS 5 | An Audit of Internal Control over Financial Reporting That Is Integrated with an Audit of Financial Statements (effective for fiscal years ending on or after November 15, 2007.) |

Now, back to the Accounting Standards Board (ASB) standards.  In addition to GAAS, the ASB has issued Statements on Auditing Standards (SAS).  These SASs are interpretations of GAAS.  Similar to the FASB Statements, the SASs are numbered sequentially as 1, 2, 3, and so on.  Some SASs are superseded and others are amended.  Therefore, the SASs are somewhat difficult to search.

To make it more convenient to find the rules, the SASs are reorganized by topic and codified in a searchable infobase.  As indicated above, the writers of the codified standards (listed as AUs, ATs, ARs, ETs, BL, QCs, etc.) have attempted to include the PCAOB material in the infobase.  However, be advised that the PCAOB has issued caution when referring to the electronic standards.  It is possible that the interim electronic standards may have been superseded by newer standards issued by the PCAOB.  Therefore, the PCAOB cautions that it is the responsibility of the individual user to make sure he or she is using the appropriate updated rules.

## STANDARDS TESTED ON THE CPA EXAM

Your head is probably swimming now.  Let's add some focus and clarification for the CPA exam.  Right now, all of this is in a state of flux because the PCAOB is a relatively new standard-setting body.  Therefore, you may see different standards from the PCAOB and the ASB on the CPA exam.  Or you may see different portions of the standards on the exam.  As the CPA exam evolves to stay current with these new PCAOB standards, the infobase may change. So, what does that mean to you on the CPA exam?

First, the CPA exam will have the appropriate version of the infobase for that testing window.  If the exam does not provide the new Auditing Standards issued by the PCAOB, then the candidate will only see questions that refer to the standards that are included on the exam.

So, that narrows it down.  If you see PCAOB standards, abbreviated AS 1, AS 2, AS 3, AS 4, and AS 5, then you could encounter a question that relates to these new standards.  If you don't see the PCAOB standards (AS 1, AS 2, etc.), you could still receive a question that involves PCAOB standards.  However, the answer would be integrated into the ASB standards on the AICPA infobase.

In any event, read the problem carefully to determine if the question involves a publicly traded company.  If not, then the regular ASB standards apply.  If it does involve a publicly traded company, then look to see if the question involves an issue that the PCAOB addressed.

Second, know the five issues on the PCAOB standards.  Those will be the "hot" topics that you need to be aware of so that you use the correct standard.  You can study these new standards within your regular audit material in your CPA review course.

## THE AICPA RESOURCE INFOBASE

Now let's focus on the organization and content of the AICPA Professional Standards.  Exhibit 6.2 is a list of the organization of the AICPA Professional Standards.

**Exhibit 6.2:  AICPA Professional Standards**

| Prefix | Topic |
|--------|-------|
| None | Applicability of AICPA Professional Standards and PCAOB Standards |
| AU | Statements on Auditing Standards and Related Auditing Interpretations |
| RULE | Select SEC-Approved PCAOB rules |
| AT | Statements on Standards for Attestation Engagements and Related Attest Engagement Interpretations |
| AR | Statements on Standards for Accounting and Review Services and Related Accounting and Review Services Interpretations |
| ET | Code of Professional Conduct |
| BL | Bylaws |
| CS | Consulting Services |
| QC | Quality Control |
| PR | Peer Review |
| TS | Tax Services |
| PFP | Personal Financial Planning |
| CPE | Continuing Professional Education |

Although you may not find all portions of the infobase on the exam, technically, the entire infobase could be tested.  As a CPA, you are required to be familiar with *all* of the professional literature.  Because the infobase is extremely large, it is possible that the AICPA may use a smaller subset of the infobase that relates more closely to the exam.  If you are familiar with all parts of the standards, then you can handle any question on any topic.

In the professional standards, it is very important that you pay close attention to the type of engagement.  You will be in a different area of the standards, depending upon the type of engagement.  For example, if a question is asked regarding evidence in an audit, you should be researching in the AUs. If the question concerns an issue for a compilation or a review, then you need to be in the ARs. Similarly, if there is a question regarding attestation, you should be in the ATs.

Again, this cannot be said emphatically enough: Make *sure* you are in the correct portion of the infobase for the type of engagement shown in the simulation!

## THE AUDITING STANDARDS—AU

As we discussed, the Auditing Standards Board issues the Statements on Auditing Standards (SAS). These SASs are codified into another publication and categorized as shown in Exhibit 6.3. At first glance, the titles in this list are not as descriptive as you would like for research. However, if you learn the numbering system for the auditing standards, the auditing rules are easy to find.

**Exhibit 6.3: Auditing Standards**

| Number | Title |
|--------|-------|
| AU 100 | Statements on Auditing Standards—Introduction |
| AU 200 | The General Standards |
| AU 300 | The Standards of Fieldwork |
| AU 400 | The First, Second, and Third Standards of Reporting |
| AU 500 | The Fourth Standard of Reporting |
| AU 600 | Other Types of Reports |
| AU 700 | Special Topics |
| AU 800 | Compliance Auditing |
| AU 900 | Special Reports of the Committee on Auditing Procedure |

Note that each number shown above is merely the category number at the highest level of organization; there are many numbers in each category that identify specific rules for the audit. For example, the AU 200 series outlines the different reports for audits. The list of sections for the AU 200 series is shown in the Exhibit 6.4. Note that this is a complete list for the 200 series. The numbers are not consecutive. The numbers skip from 201 to 210.

**Exhibit 6.4: Auditing Standards 200 Series, The General Standards**

| Number | Title |
|--------|-------|
| 201 | Nature of the General Standards |
| 210 | Training and Proficiency of the Independent Auditor |
| 220 | Independence |
| 230 | Due Professional Care in the Performance of Work |

In some areas of the standards, interpretations are necessary. These interpretations are found in the 9000 series immediately after the rule. Notice the last three digits match the standard number. The 9 in front denotes that it is an interpretation. A list of contents with the interpretations in the 500 series would be organized as shown in Exhibit 6.5. Notice that not all sections have an interpretation.

**Exhibit 6.5: Auditing Standards and Interpretations Example of Organization**

| Number | Title |
|--------|-------|
| 504 | Association with Financial Statements |
| 9504 | Association with Financial Statements:  Auditing Interpretations of Section 504 |
| 508 | Reports on Audited Financial Statements |
| 9508 | Reports on Audited Financial Statements:  Auditing Interpretations of  Section 508 |
| 530 | Dating of the Independent Auditor's Report |
| 532 | Restricting the Use of an Auditor's Report |
| 534 | Reporting on Financial Statements Prepared for Use in Other Countries |
| 9534 | Reporting on Financial Statements Prepared for Use in Other Countries:  Auditing Interpretations of Section 534 |

Let's make a few more observations here. First, the titles at this level are very descriptive. When you click on a section, such as AU 500, you will see the detailed sections in the 500 series. If you click further down to the most detailed level of a standard, you will see the section number and the paragraph number, such as AU 504.02.

The section number and paragraph number are the level that you will be citing in the research component on the CPA exam. However, you will not be required to type in the citation number. Instead, you will click on that paragraph, the paragraph will be highlighted, and you will go to the upper left-hand portion of the research screen, and click on "Transfer to Answer"—and you're done! The software automatically transfers your answer to the research solution window. Be sure to read the instructions carefully to see if the answer requires one paragraph or more than one paragraph. Also, be sure to read Chapters 8 and 9 before the AUD exam so you fully understand how the research infobase works.

As we discuss in Chapter 9, the screen must be split with both the standards and the research tabs open or the answer will not highlight and transfer. Be sure to read Chapter 9 and the additional materials in Appendix C that explain the exam interface and commands in more detail.

## A CLOSER LOOK AT THE AUDITING STANDARDS

Let's spend a little more time with these auditing standards. Let's take our list of Auditing Standards, and look at these numbers more closely. We need to examine the titles that go with these numbers and group them in a way that is easy to remember. Exhibit 6.6 is a study list of the auditing standards.

**Exhibit 6.6: Auditing Standards Study List**

| Number | Title |
|--------|-------|
| AU 100 | Statements on Auditing Standards—Introduction |
| AU 200 | The General Standards |
| AU 300 | The Standards of Fieldwork |
| AU 400 | The First, Second, and Third Standards of Reporting |
| AU 500 | The Fourth Standard of Reporting |
| AU 600 | Other Types of Reports |
| AU 700 | Special Topics |
| AU 800 | Compliance Auditing |
| AU 900 | Special Reports of the Committee on Auditing Procedures |

AU 100 and AU 200 can be viewed as setting the stage for the audit environment. AU 100 is relatively short and identifies the responsibilities and functions of the auditor, generally accepted auditing standards, and the relationship of these auditing standards to quality control standards. Exhibit 6.7 is a list of topics in the AU 100 series.

**Exhibit 6.7: Auditing Standards 100 Series**

| Number | Title |
|--------|-------|
| 110 | Responsibilities and Functions of the Independent Auditor |
| 120 | Defining Professional Requirements in Statements on Auditing Standards |
| 150 | Generally Accepted Auditing Standards |
| 161 | The Relationship of Generally Accepted Auditing Standards to Quality Control Standards |

AU 200 addresses the nature of the general standards, the training and proficiency of the auditor, and the requirements for independence and due professional care. Exhibit 6.8 outlines the titles of standards in the AU 200 series.

**Exhibit 6.8: Auditing Standards 200 Series**

| Number | Title |
|--------|-------|
| 201 | Nature of the General Standards |
| 210 | Training and Proficiency of the Independent Auditor |
| 220 | Independence |
| 230 | Due Professional Care in the Performance of Work |

The AU 300 series begins to address the actual work of the auditor—that's why it's titled the Standards of Fieldwork. Exhibit 6.9 outlines the AU 300 series. The 9000 interpretations have been omitted from the list.

Slowly and carefully read this list.  Give particular attention to the types of topics included in the AU 300 series.

**Exhibit 6.9:  Auditing Standards 300 Series**

| Number | Title |
|---|---|
| 310 | Appointment of the Independent Auditor |
| 311 | Planning and Supervision |
| 312 | Audit Risk and Materiality |
| 313 | Substantive Tests prior to the Balance Sheet Date |
| 314 | Understanding the Entity and Its Environment and Assessing the Risks of Material Misstatement |
| 315 | Communications between Predecessor and Successor Auditors |
| 316 | Consideration of Fraud in a Financial Statement Audit |
| 317 | Illegal Acts by Clients |
| 318 | Performing Audit Procedures in Response to Assessed Risks and Evaluating the Audit Evidence Obtained |
| 319 | Consideration of Internal Control in Financial Statement Audit |
| 322 | Auditor's Consideration of the Internal Audit Function in an Audit of Financial Statements |
| 324 | Service Organizations |
| 325 | Communication of Internal Control Related Matters Noted in Audit |
| 326 | Audit Evidence |
| 328 | Auditing Fair Value Measurements and Disclosures |
| 329 | Analytical Procedures |
| 330 | The Confirmation Process |
| 331 | Inventories |
| 332 | Auditing Derivative Instruments, Hedging Activities, and Investments in Securities |
| 333 | Management Representations |
| 334 | Related Parties |
| 336 | Using the Work of a Specialist |
| 337 | Inquiry of a Client's Lawyer Concerning Litigation, Claims, and Assessments |
| 339 | Audit Documentation |
| 341 | The Auditor's Consideration of an Entity's Ability to Continue as a Going Concern |
| 342 | Auditing Accounting Estimates |
| 350 | Audit Sampling |
| 380 | The Auditor's Communication with Those Charged with Governance |
| 390 | Consideration of Omitted Procedures after the Report Date |

This is a very large standard that addresses appointment of the auditor, engagement planning, audit risk and materiality, substantive tests, fraud, illegal acts, internal control, internal audit, evidence, analytical procedures, confirmations—all the rules pertaining to doing the audit work. How to, how to, how to! These are the rules for how to conduct the audit.

The AU 300 series is very large. Fortunately, the drop-down menu titles are very descriptive, and these menus will guide you to your research topic. Be patient, and keep drilling down into the table of contents. It's a detailed *how to* series.

The 300 series has long titles. When you are researching, you should open your table of contents window *wide* to read the titles. You will also see that the 300 series is interspersed heavily with the 9000s for interpretations. If the interpretations are included in the infobase on the CPA exam, do not let the 9000s bother you. Stay focused on the titles of the standards and dig down through those menus.

The AU 400 series is titled the first, second, and third standards of reporting. Interesting, because one would think that the numbering system would align with the $1^{st}$, $2^{nd}$, and $3^{rd}$ in the title, and these would be in a 100, 200 and 300 series. This is not the case. The numbering system is not linked to the $1^{st}$, $2^{nd}$, $3^{rd}$, or $4^{th}$ standard of reporting.

The first, second, and third standard of reporting are all the in the 400 series. The 400 series addresses adherence to GAAP, consistent application of GAAP, adequacy of disclosures in financial statements, and segment information. The rules here address the issues of changes in reporting entity, change or error in principle, changes in classification, reclassifications, and so on. It deals with the standards of reporting, *not* the audit report itself.

The 400 series is rather short, with only five sections. Just remember this section addresses adherence to GAAP and adequate disclosures that comply with GAAP. Exhibit 6.10 outlines the 400 series of the auditing standards.

**Exhibit 6.10: Auditing Standards 400 Series, the First, Second, and Third Standards of Reporting**

| Number | Title |
|--------|-------|
| 410 | Adherence to GAAP |
| 411 | The Meaning of Present Fairly in Conformity with GAAP |
| 420 | Consistency of Application of GAAP |
| 431 | Adequacy of Disclosure in Financial Statements |
| 435 | Segment Information (Rescinded by the Auditing Standards Board) |

The AU 500 series, the fourth standard of reporting, addresses the actual audit report. This section also provides examples of audit reports for the various types of opinions, (i.e. standard report, qualified opinion, adverse opinion, and disclaimer of opinion). It is further detailed into sample paragraphs for issues ranging from scope limitations, lack of consistency, inadequate disclosures, or going concern problems.

An important point is that the PCAOB reporting requirements are included in this section. Near the end of AU 508, you will find the sample paragraphs for reports that conform to the new PCAOB rules. These PCAOB rules should be interspersed into the infobase at the appropriate locations.

Exhibit 6.11 outlines the 500 series of the auditing standards. Again, remember that the 500 series focuses on the actual audit report.

**Exhibit 6.11:  Auditing Standards 500 Series**

| Number | Title |
|--------|-------|
| 504 | Association with Financial Statements |
| 508 | Reports on Audited Financial Statements |
| 530 | Dating of the Independent Auditor's Report |
| 532 | Restricting the User of an Auditor's Report |
| 534 | Reporting on Financial Statements Prepared for Use in Other Countries |
| 543 | Part of Audit Performed by Other Independent Auditors |
| 544 | Lack of Conformity with Generally Accepted Accounting Principles |
| 550 | Other Information in Documents Containing Audited Financial Statements |
| 551 | Reporting on Information Accompanying the Basic Financial Statements in Auditor-Submitted Documents |
| 552 | Reporting on Condensed Financial Statements and Selected Financial Data |
| 558 | Required Supplementary Information |
| 560 | Subsequent Events |
| 561 | Subsequent Discovery of Facts Existing at the Date of the Auditor's Report |

Now, back away from this. The order of the auditing standards makes perfect sense. First, we begin with the big picture, and who is doing the audit (100 and 200), then it's *how* you do it (300), whether it complies with GAAP (400), and making the report (500). The AUs have a very nice organizational structure!

## THE ATTESTATION STANDARDS

The attestation standards are organized by type of engagement or work being performed. In other words, what is being attested to? Depending on *what* the attestation involves, the rules can be different.

There are nine basic standards for attestations, and these are numbered AT 20 through AT 701. AT 20 and AT 50 outline the professional requirements and the Statements on Standards for Attestation Engagements (SSAE) hierarchy. Starting with AT 101, each standard usually begins with objectives and definitions, and then moves into the details of how to conduct that part of the attestation. Again, with the attestation standards, first be sure to focus on *what* is being attesting to, and then look for the *how to* rules. Exhibit 6.12 outlines the Attestation Standards.

**Exhibit 6.12: Attestation Engagements Study List**

| Number | Title |
|--------|-------|
| AT 20 | Defining Professional Requirements in Statements on Standards for Attestation Engagements |
| AT 50 | SSAE Hierarchy |
| AT 101 | Attest Engagements |
| AT 201 | Agreed-Upon Procedures Engagements |
| AT 301 | Financial Forecasts and Projections |
| AT 401 | Reporting on Pro Forma Financial Information |
| AT 501 | Reporting on an Entity's Internal Control over Financial Reporting |
| AT 601 | Compliance Attestation |
| AT 701 | Management's Discussion and Analysis |

Again, once you are in the attestation standards, each type of attestation will have its own rules. Dig down into the appropriate standard for the type of attestation being performed.

## THE ACCOUNTING AND REVIEW STANDARDS

The Statements on Standards for Accounting and Review Services (SSARS) have also been codified and are listed as AR. Pay specific attention to these, as historically many CPA questions have been taken from this area of the standards. Be careful here! There is a big difference between a compilation and a review, so read the question carefully. Exhibit 6.13 outlines major headings in the Accounting and Review Standards.

**Exhibit 6.13: Accounting and Review Services Study List**

| Number | Title |
|--------|-------|
| AR 50 | Standards for Accounting and Review Services |
| AR 100 | Compilation and Review of Financial Statements |
| AR 110 | Compilation of Specified Elements, Accounts, or Items of a Financial Statement |
| AR 120 | Compilation of Pro Forma Financial Information |
| AR 200 | Reporting on Comparative Financial Statements |
| AR 300 | Compilation Reports on Financial Statements Included in Certain Prescribed Forms |
| AR 400 | Communications between Predecessor and Successor Accountants |
| AR 600 | Reporting on Personal Financial Statements Included in Written Personal Financial Plans |

## STRATEGIES FOR AUDITING RESEARCH

Although you might think there is only one research question in each simulation, this may not be the case for the auditing section of the exam. In addition to a research requirement, the simulations may also contain a "reporting" requirement. This reporting requirement will require you to use the AICPA infobase to cut and paste the appropriate paragraphs for some type of report. You may be required to cut and paste up to ten paragraphs in this section of the exam. Therefore, it is *imperative* that you know your way around the AICPA infobase. Research on this infobase can affect not just one part, but potentially *two* parts of a simulation!

Whether you are answering a general research question or you are compiling some type of report or letter, the first goal is to identify the type of work being done: audit, attestation, compilation, review, consulting, or tax work. Each type of work has standards in a different location in the infobase.

Once you know you are in the correct portion of the infobase, you can then start dropping down the section titles and looking for the correct topic. When you find the appropriate topic or area, scroll through that standard and skim quickly. If it is a section that is particularly long, you can use the *search within* command. If you plan to use the *search* commands, be sure to practice the *search* and *search within* commands on the sample CPA exam *before* you take the exam. Practice these searches many times until you are competent and fast at retrieving information. Remember, on the CPA exam, it is a race against the clock, and you must be proficient with your search techniques.

## THE EXAM INTERFACE FOR AUDITING AND ATTESTATION

If you examine the sample exam closely, the research for Auditing and Attestation appears to be slightly different from FAR or REG. For example, on the sample exam, the audit research component indicates that a citation may include one paragraph or more than one paragraph. Candidates must highlight each appropriate paragraph and transfer each paragraph to the answer window. After the paragraphs have been transferred to the answer window, the order of the paragraphs may be rearranged. Practice this technique on the sample exam so that you are proficient with the commands for rearranging your answer.

The audit section is unlike FAR or REG, where the candidate selects only one paragraph, highlights it, and transfers it to the answer window. In FAR or REG, if a second paragraph is selected, the new selection replaces the previous paragraph transferred to the answer.

At first, it appeared that only the "report" portion of the simulation in auditing required an answer with multiple paragraphs. However, after careful analysis of the auditing simulations on the sample exam, it appears the

exam may also require the candidate to cut and paste more than one paragraph in the research area.  Be sure to read Chapter 9 for additional information on the simulations and research components on the exam.

Finally, it's important to check the CPA exam Web page at www.cpa-
exam.org for any special instructions or last-minute updates on the
functionality of the exam.  Simulation version 1.5 was launched in April
2006.  This newer version of the simulation interface appears to be easier to
use than the original interface.

When CPA candidates experience difficulty with a particular function,
the AICPA has been very responsive by posting special instructions on their
Web page.  It is always wise to check the AICPA Web page for any of these
announcements approximately seven to ten days before taking each section
of the exam to make *sure* there are no changes or special instructions for the
exam interface.

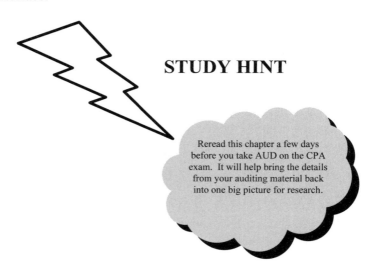

## STUDY HINT

Reread this chapter a few days
before you take AUD on the CPA
exam.  It will help bring the details
from your auditing material back
into one big picture for research.

## TEST YOURSELF

**1.** In what area of the auditing standards are the standards for issuing the audit report?

    a.   AU 200 series.
    b.   AU 300 series.
    c.   AU 400 series.
    d.   AU 500 series.

**2.** In what area of the auditing standards will the standards on how to conduct an audit be found?

    a.   AU 100 series.
    b.   AU 200 series.
    c.   AU 300 series.
    d.   AU 500 series.

**3.** The first, second, and third standard of reporting contained in the AU 400 series includes which of the following information?

    a.   Proficiency of the auditor.
    b.   Consistent application of GAAP.
    c.   Independence of the auditor.
    d.   Audit risk and materiality.

**4.** The fourth standard of reporting addresses which issue?

    a.   Proficiency of the auditor.
    b.   The exercise of due care.
    c.   Substantive tests prior to the balance sheet date.
    d.   Reports on audited financial statements.

**5.** The rules for subsequent events would be found in which location in the auditing standards?

    a.   AU 100 series.
    b.   AU 300 series.
    c.   AU 400 series.
    d.   AU 500 series.

**6.** The auditing standards that address evidential matter are contained in which area of the infobase?

    a.   AU 200 series.
    b.   AU 300 series.
    c.   AU 400 series.
    d.   AU 500 series.

**7.** A 9000 series number indicates which of the following?

    a.   An auditing standard.
    b.   An attestation standard.
    c.   A compilation and review standard.
    d.   An interpretation of a standard.

**8.** Which of the following abbreviations is used in the standards for a compilation and review?

    a.   AR.
    b.   CR.
    c.   AU.
    d.   AT.

**9.** Which of the following abbreviations is used in the standards that include the code of professional conduct for CPAs?

    a.   PC.
    b.   RULE.
    c.   ET.
    d.   QC.

**10.** Which of the following abbreviations is used in the standards to identify the rules for attestation engagements?

    a.   AE.
    b.   AT.
    c.   AR.
    d.   AU.

## PRACTICE YOUR RESEARCH SKILLS

1.  In an audit, what must an auditor understand about the entity?

2.  What are the components of risk regarding the risk of material misstatement in an audit?

3.  What is a compilation of a financial statement?

4.  In an audit, what is an adverse opinion?

5.  In an audit, what is fraud and how does it differ from an accounting error?

6.  What are the five areas of internal control in the auditing standards?

7.  What are the two types of sampling risks when performing substantive tests in auditing?

8.  A CPA is asked to attest to prospective financial statements. What are the two types of uses for prospective financial statements?

9.  For purposes of assessing internal controls in an audit, what is a control deficiency?

10. Why are analytical procedures used in an audit?

# 7 TAX RESEARCH

For many people, tax research might seem overwhelming. Perhaps you have never looked at the code. Perhaps you don't want to! Or perhaps you have, and you remember all that tiny print and those horrible footnotes at the bottom of the page. Not to worry! The CPA exam only requires that you give the code section and paragraph number. We'll look at how the code is organized and the areas of tax that are most likely to be tested. We'll establish some useful vocabulary for finding the correct answer. Of course, this chapter won't make you an expert tax researcher in all of the tax resources, but it should be enough to get you through the CPA exam!

## THE INTERNAL REVENUE CODE

First, let's talk about taxes in general. In the tax arena, the Code is the LAW. The Code contains the laws passed by Congress and signed by the President of the United States. The Regulations (often called Regs) are interpretations of the code and guidance provided by the Treasury Department. There are also Revenue Rulings that rule on a specific client's issue. For right now, on the CPA exam, you don't have to worry about the regulations or the revenue rulings because they are not on the exam. Tax gurus from a masters in taxation program can relax because the focus on the CPA exam is on the Code and Publication 17.

The Code is referred to as IRC—the Internal Revenue Code. The Internal Revenue Service is the branch of the Treasury Department that administers and ensures compliance with the tax laws. Do not confuse the initials IRC and IRS. For the research component, you'll be citing the Internal Revenue Code, or IRC sections.

You have studied for the Regulations component; you know your tax rules. However, *finding* a rule in the Code may feel like finding a needle in a haystack. Don't worry! Believe it or not, the Code is organized in a rather useful way.

## ORGANIZATION OF THE CODE

First, let's look at the Code in its entirety. Notice that the Code contains more than the laws for income tax. The Code contains all of the tax laws for the various types of taxes levied in the US The Internal Revenue Code is divided into subtitles. The subtitles are established for each of the different types of taxes, as well as other laws pertaining to taxation. Exhibit 7.1 identifies the subtitles of the Code.

**Exhibit 7.1: Title 26 Internal Revenue Code**

| Subtitle | Topic |
|---|---|
| A | Income Taxes |
| B | Estate and Gift Taxes |
| C | Employment Taxes |
| D | Miscellaneous Excise Taxes |
| E | Alcohol, Tobacco, and Miscellaneous Taxes |
| F | Procedure and Administration |
| G | The Joint Committee on Taxation |
| H | Financing of the Presidential Election Campaigns |
| I | Trust Fund Code |
| J | Coal Industry Health Benefits |
| K | Group Health Plan Requirements |

For the CPA exam, our focus will be on Subtitle A—Income Taxes, Subtitle B—Estate and Gift Taxes, and Subtitle F—Procedure and Administration.

Within each subtitle, the Code is broken in chapters. Within Subtitle A—Income Taxes, there are six chapters. Although theoretically the exam could ask any research question, we will focus on the areas most likely to be tested. Chapter 1—Normal Taxes and Surtaxes is most likely to be tested on the CPA exam. Exhibit 7.2 outlines the chapters of Subtitle A—Income Taxes.

**Exhibit 7.2: Internal Revenue Code Subtitle A—Income Taxes**

| Chapter 1 | Normal Taxes and Surtaxes |
|---|---|
| Chapter 2 | Tax on Self-Employment Income |
| Chapter 3 | Withholding of Tax on Nonresident Aliens and Foreign Corporations |
| Chapter 4 | Repealed |
| Chapter 5 | Repealed |
| Chapter 6 | Consolidated Returns |

The chapters are further divided into subchapters that are alphabetically organized, A through Y. In subchapters, the content is divided by topic. Pay particular attention to the groupings here. You don't need to memorize these, but you need to be able to "feel" where things are. For example, it is helpful to know that partnerships are "in the middle"—Subchapter K.

Exhibit 7.3 lists the subchapters of Chapter 1 of Subtitle A—Income Taxes. Carefully read this list, making a mental note of the special interest areas. For the CPA exam, the most important subchapters in this list are Subchapters A, B, C, D, E, J, K, O, P, and S. So, we've narrowed our studying down a bit already.

**Exhibit 7.3:  Internal Revenue Code Subtitle A—Income Taxes**
**Chapter 1—Normal Taxes and Surtaxes**

| Subchapter | Topic |
|---|---|
| A | Determination of Tax Liability |
| BTP | Computation of Taxable Income |
| CHF | Corporate Distributions and Adjustments |
| D | Deferred Compensation, etc. |
| EBITDA | Accounting Periods and Methods of Accounting |
| F | Exempt Organizations |
| Group | Corporations Used to Avoid Income Tax on Shareholders |
| H | Banking Institutions |
| I | Natural Resources |
| J | Estates, Trusts, Beneficiaries, and Decedents |
| K | Partners and Partnerships |
| L | Insurance Companies |
| M | Regulated Investment Companies and Real Estate Investment Trusts |
| N | Tax Based on Income from Sources within or without the United States |
| O | Gain or Loss on Disposition of Property |
| P | Capital Gains and Losses |
| Q | Readjustment of Tax between Years and Special Limitations |
| R | Repealed |
| S | Tax Treatment of S Corporations and Their Shareholders |
| T | Cooperatives and Their Patrons |
| U | Designation and Treatment of Empowerment Zones, Enterprise Communities, and Rural Development Investment Areas |
| V | Title 11 Cases |
| W | District of Columbia Enterprise Zone |
| X | Renewal Communities |
| Y | New York Liberty Zone Benefits |

Within each subchapter, there are parts. These parts are clearly labeled on the table of contents. Therefore, the table of contents is an excellent tool to find the answer to a research question. Within each part, there are section numbers. In the code, the section number is marked "Sec. 162" but in tax lingo, it is written with the section symbol "§." You may see this symbol on the CPA exam.

Each code section is divided into paragraphs such as (a), (b), or (c). Then the paragraphs can have subparagraphs labeled with numbers in parentheses, (1), (2), (3). Those subparagraphs can be divided further, and then again further. At this point, we are at a level of detail beyond what the exam will test.

Let's briefly review.  If we diagram the organization of the Code, you can see a more understandable structure of the Code.  Exhibit 7.4 identifies the outline or structure of the Code.  Notice how each piece of the code is marked in the notation.  Notice the differences in capital letters, Roman numerals, numbers without parentheses, and lower case letters, numbers, capital letters, and lowercase and uppercase roman numerals in parentheses.

**Exhibit 7.4:  Organization of the Code**

```
Subtitle A
   Chapter 1
      Subchapter B
         Part        II
            Section    71
               Subsection (f)
                  Paragraph  (3)
                     Subparagraph (B)
                        Clause          (i)
                           Subclause      (II)
```

At this point, you're probably thinking, "what a mess!"  But I have great news for you!  You really don't need to worry about any of that, because when you open up the Code on the CPA exam, you will see Subchapters with titles, and then you will expand your table of contents and delve down into each layer by clicking on the title.  Actually, it's quite easy!  Get online with an infobase or get online with the sample exam and try it!

Let's look at that giant outline one more time in Exhibit 7.5.  This time we'll mark in bold the part that is important to you for the CPA exam.

**Exhibit 7.5: IRC—Table of Contents for CPA Exam**

```
Subtitle A
   Chapter 1
      Subchapter P
         Part        I
            Section    175
               Subsection   (a)
                  Paragraph
                     Subparagraph
                        Clause
                           Subclause
```

On the CPA exam, what will you need to cite?  You will only need to cite the code section and the paragraph, such as §162 (a).  Remember, paragraph references are small letters, not capital letters.

You won't need to cite the subchapter or part, but you will have to go through those menus to find your answer.  In addition, even though you may find your answer at the (1)(i) level, the entire section and subsection may highlight and transfer to your answer.

If you don't use the table of contents to look for titles, your other choice, of course, is to use a keyword search. Again, it is likely that if your vocabulary is not tax-perfect, you may find no results or too many results to read through in the short amount of time available. Keep in mind, though, if you don't hit the vocabulary head-on, you won't find it. If you cannot find your issue with a keyword search, try again with the table of contents. If you understand how the tax code is organized, using the table of contents menus is faster and easier than keyword searches.

When you find your answer, you will click on the appropriate paragraph, highlight it, and then click "Transfer to Answer." Your answer will be transferred to the answer window on your exam. The exam software will transfer the appropriate citation, code section, paragraph, et cetera. Depending on the programming of the exam during your particular testing window, it should transfer the entire paragraph to the answer window. Version 1.5 of the simulation transfers the entire paragraph to the answer window.

Even though the code looks overwhelming at first, you need only to focus on the organization of the code sections. Research in the Code is relatively straightforward because the numbering system does *not* reuse the section numbers from subchapter to subchapter. As you progress through each subchapter of the Code, the section numbers become larger. Let's look at our list again, and now we'll add the section number ranges to the subchapter headings. This list has been shortened to include the most important subchapters.

When you study, focus on the section numbers of the code. As the section numbers increase, you'll notice you are moving into different subchapters. The subchapters will be clearly labeled, so you shouldn't have a problem deciding which subchapter to open up in the table of contents. Exhibit 7.6 lists the code sections and topics.

**Exhibit 7.6:  Internal Revenue Code List of Code Sections Subtitle A–
Chapter 1**

| Subchapter | Topic | Sections |
|---|---|---|
| A | Determination of Tax Liability | §1-59 |
| BTP | Computation of Taxable Income | §61-291 |
| CHF | Corporate Distributions and Adjustments | §300's |
| D | Deferred Compensation, etc. | §401-424 |
| EBITDA | Accounting Periods and Methods of Accounting | §441-483 |
| F | Exempt Organizations | §501-528 |
| Group | Corporations Used to Avoid Income Tax on Shareholders | §531-565 |
| H | Banking Institutions | §581-591 |

| Subchapter | Topic | Sections |
|:---:|:---|:---|
| I | Natural Resources | §611-638 |
| J | Estates, Trusts, Beneficiaries, and Decedents | §641-692 |
| K | Partners and Partnerships | §700's |
| L | Insurance Companies | §801-841 |
| M | Regulated Investment Companies and Real Estate Investment Trusts | §851-860 |
| N | Tax Based on Income from Sources within or without the United States | §861-999 |
| O | Gain or Loss on Disposition of Property | §1001-1092 |
| P | Capital Gains and Losses | §1200's |
| Q | Readjustment of Tax between Years and Special Limitations | §1300-1351 |
| S | Tax Treatment of S Corporations and Their Shareholders | §131-1379 |
| T | Cooperatives and Their Patrons | §1381-1388 |

Carefully read Exhibit 7.6. Notice that everything is grouped by topic. Now let's shorten the list to include only the topics that are most likely to be tested. Exhibit 7.7 is a shortened list of the most important topics.

**Exhibit 7.7: Internal Revenue Code Income Taxes Quick Study List**

| Subchapter | Topic | Section Numbers |
|:---:|:---|:---|
| A | Determination of Tax Liability | §1-59 |
| BTP | Computation of Taxable Income | §61-291 |
| CHF | Corporate Distributions and Adjustments | §300's |
| D | Deferred Compensation, etc. | §401-424 |
| EBITDA | Accounting Periods and Methods of Accounting | §441-483 |
| F | Exempt Organizations | §501-530 |
| Group | Corporations Used to Avoid Income Tax on Shareholders | §531-565 |
| J | Estates, Trusts, Beneficiaries, and Decedents | §641-692 |
| K | Partners and Partnerships | §700's |
| N | Tax Based on Income from Sources within or without the United States | §861-999 |
| O | Gain or Loss on Disposition of Property | §1000's |
| P | Capital Gains and Losses | §1200's |
| Q | Readjustment of Tax between Years and Special Limitations | §1301-1351 |
| S | Tax Treatment of S Corporations and Their Shareholders | §1361-1379 |

Now let's focus on each subchapter. We'll review the basics of the contents in each subchapter. Keep in mind, the subchapters are grouped by topic. Sometimes, the organization of the Code is not completely intuitive. For example, you might think that all individual taxation is in one chapter, and corporation taxation is in another chapter. However, this is not the case. The Code is not organized by type of organization, but rather by tax topics. Some tax rules apply to several different organizations, such as individuals, Schedule-C filers, partnerships, corporations, and S Corporations. In other words, it doesn't matter what kind of business you have, depreciation applies to all businesses. Therefore, the Code is not grouped by business organization.

You must be asking, "if the Code is not organized by type of organization, how *is* the Code organized? Let's analyze each subchapter in more depth.

### Subchapter A, §1-59

This area of the Code deals with *who* gets taxed and how much. In other words, Section 1-59 contains the laws that establish the government's right to tax individuals, corporations, and other entities. This is also where the tax rates and tax tables are found. Subchapter A also has some basic definitions of tax liability, credits against tax, foreign tax credits, earned income credits, and AMT taxes. Remember, a tax credit directly reduces the tax paid. So it makes sense that tax credits are grouped with calculating the tax due the government. Remember, Sections 1-59 of the Code deals with calculating the tax due.

### Subchapter B, §60-291

This is a fairly large area of the Code that addresses determining taxable income. Remember, you need to know *what* taxable income is before you can calculate the tax due in the previous section.

Subchapter B is where we find all of the important rules such as the definition of gross income, adjusted gross income, deductions, exclusions, personal exemptions, and alimony. This area deals with anything related to calculating taxable income. More importantly, this area of the code relates to any individual or business, regardless of the form of organization. Remember our friend, §162, Trade or Business Expenses, the ordinary and necessary requirement? Depreciation deductions, medical expenses, personal deductions, casualty loss deductions, charitable contributions—it's all here! Just delve down into the table of contents on Subchapter B and keep looking for your topic.

Other highlights—§195—start-up expenditures are here. The dividends received deduction (DRD) is here in §243. You would think that DRD would be somewhere in corporate material, but DRD is here! Why? Because it is a deduction. Another surprise in this section is §267 on related taxpayers. Remember in GAAP, we were always concerned with related-party transactions? Well, so is the US Government—but notice the vocabulary is different from GAAP. The Code does not refer to it as related-party transactions, but related taxpayers. Keyword searches are likely to need a vocabulary adjustment in the tax area. Pay specific attention to tax vocabulary as you study for REG. Put your tax hat on and think tax!

### Subchapter C, §300s

Subchapter C addresses corporate distributions and adjustments. Interestingly, the tax rates for corporations are in Subchapter A, the rules for what to include in income are in Subchapter B, but C is very special. And C stands for *corporation*! Some of the more important features of the Subchapter C area include corporate distributions, liquidations, organizations and reorganizations, insolvent corporations, NOL carryover rules, stock basis rules, and debt vs. equity issues. Loads of fun here!

### Subchapter D, §421–424

Subchapter D covers deferred compensation. Although, in theory, deferred compensation could be tested on the CPA exam, this might be considered too detailed or special interest. Although the individuals who designed the Code may not have intended it this way, remember D stands for Deferred Compensation. Make a mental note of that, just in case you encounter a research question.

### Subchapter E, §441-483

Subchapter E is important. This is the area of the Code that addresses calendar years, fiscal year ends, changing accounting periods, returns for periods of less than 12 months, and election of a tax year. You need to know where this is.

Subchapter E is also the area of the Code that addresses permissible accounting methods (cash receipts and disbursements method, accrual method), installment method of income, when to include prepaid income, and rules for long-term contracts. This section also includes those rules for taxable year of deduction.

Let's compare and contrast here. Subchapter B told us *how much* to include in income, but Subchapter E tells us *when* to put it in income.

Some interesting topics in this chapter include the passive activity limitations, inventory valuation, allocation of income and deductions, and the requirement of clearly reflecting income. These issues involve the timing of claiming certain income and losses. Therefore, timing issues are found in E in §441-483. All of these are hot topics.

## Subchapter F, §531-565

Subchapter F covers exempt organizations.  Subchapter F of the Code identifies the qualifications to be classified as an exempt organization.  Here you will find the general rules and requirements for exempt organizations, private foundations, farmer cooperatives, political organizations, homeowners associations, and higher education savings entities.  In addition, the rules for taxation of business income of certain exempt organizations for unrelated business income are found in Subchapter F.

## Subchapter G, §531-565

The title to Subchapter G is long:  Corporations Used to Avoid Income Tax on Shareholders.  In plain English, these rules are commonly referred to in tax class as earnings and profits (E&P).  In tax language, Subchapter G contains the rules for the accumulated earnings tax for those corporations that improperly accumulate surplus.

Subchapter G also addresses the personal holding company tax, definition of a personal holding company, rules for determining stock ownership, and undistributed personal holding income.

Another area of Subchapter G addresses the deduction for dividends paid.  Do not confuse this with the dividends *received* deduction found in §243.  These rules are very different.

## Subchapter K, §700s

The beauty of Subchapter K is that it is all about partnerships.  Subchapter K contains the rules for the income and credits for partners, partnership computations for income and deductions, distributive share, basis of partnership interests, taxable year of partner and partnership, transactions between the partner and the partnership, contributions, distributions, and transfers, and payment to retiring partners.  Everything on partnerships is here.

An interesting point about partnerships is that partnerships have some extra special rules.  Although in other forms of organization, the income and deduction rules of Subchapter B apply, Subchapter K changes some of the deduction rules as they relate to partnerships.  For example, partnerships cannot take a deduction for charitable contributions or net operating losses.  Instead, these deductions must be included on the partner's individual tax return.  So when doing research, it is wise to review those special exceptions.  Then if you encounter a partnership question, you will know to research in the 700 series for these exceptions.  The code sections for these exceptions are clearly labeled and easy to find.

### Subchapter O, §1000s

Subchapter O is property transactions. The rules for property transactions affect many different taxpayers.

There are several important issues with regard to property transactions. The first issue is gain or loss. Then, there is basis: basis if you received the property from a decedent, basis if you received the property by gift, adjustments to basis. Basis, basis, basis. That's an important topic for tax—BASIS.

Next, we have all the fun with exchanges of property. Here the Code is very specific as to conditions—whether the property was held for productive use or investment, exchanged for stock, an involuntary conversion, a gain on a principal residence, stock for stock, wash sales, transfers between spouses or in divorce, and so forth.

Remember, Subchapter O and the §1000 series focus on the gain or loss and the basis for property transactions.

### Subchapter P, §1200 series

Of course, it's not enough to know whether there is a gain or loss, a taxpayer also must know how to treat that gain or loss for tax purposes. Subchapter P is where the 1200 series is found. Subchapter P is where the rules for capital gains and capital losses are found. In addition, all of the fun recapture rules from §1245 are here too! The 1200 section of the code addresses *how* the gain or loss is taxed (i.e., as ordinary income, capital gain, or capital loss). Remember, how it is taxed is an important issue as it may affect the tax rate used to calculate the tax.

### Subchapter Q, §1301-1351

Subchapter Q addresses readjustment of tax between years and special limitations. It outlines the rules for mitigation of effect of limitations, correction of error, circumstances of adjustment, amount, and method of adjustment.

### Subchapter S, §1361-1379

Once again, we get a study hint with this section. S Corporations are called S Corporations because their rules belong to Subchapter S of the Internal Revenue Code. Keep in mind, S Corps are special, so if you're dealing with S Corps, make sure you look here for their special rules. All of the special rules such as electing S status, pass-through items to shareholders, adjustments to basis, and distributions are found in Subchapter S.

## OTHER IMPORTANT SUBTITLES

We have successfully covered Subtitle A, Income Taxes, of the Internal Revenue Code. Do not confuse the subtitles with subchapters. Remember that a subtitle is the higher level of the law that categorizes the topic of that particular set of laws, such as income tax, gift and estate tax, or alcohol and tobacco taxes. When searching, open the subtitle first, then select a chapter, and then select a subchapter. Now we need to examine Subtitles B—Gift and Estate Taxes, and Subtitle F—Procedure and Administration.

## Subtitle B—Estate and Gift Tax

There are two areas of the code that have tax laws related to estates. Subtitle A, Income Taxes, Subchapter J addresses taxing the *income* of an estate or trust, as well as income in respect of decedents. Recall that this was in §642-692 of the Code. Subtitle B addresses an entirely different issue. Subtitle B addresses the actual estate. Subtitle B establishes the rules for identifying the gross estate and the taxable estate, the imposition of tax and the tax rate, valuation of the estate, transfers at death, etc. These laws are in the 2000 series of the Code. Watch out for this!

If you have a question concerning income of the estate, go to the income tax rules in Subtitle A. If you have a question regarding estate tax, gift tax, tax on generation-skipping transfers, or valuation rules, go to the §2000 series. The estate laws are in 2000-2210. The gift taxes are in the §2500 series. The tax on generation-skipping transfers is in the §2600 series. The tax on special valuation rules is in the §2700 series. Remember, Subtitle B focuses on the *transfer* of the gift or estate.

## Subtitle F—Procedure and Administration

Again, this is an important area of the code that deals with procedure and administration. Procedure and administration addresses information and returns, time and place for paying tax, and assessment and collection of tax. It includes the rules for extension of time for filing, interest on underpayments, and penalties for failure to file tax return or pay the tax due. Furthermore, this area of the Code outlines penalties for fraudulent returns. This area of the Code also contains the rules addressing burden of proof and tax evasion issues.

The titles in the §6000 and §7000 series are very descriptive. If you encounter a research question that deals with information returns, procedures, tax administration, penalties, and judicial proceedings, be sure to look here.

## PUBLICATION 17

Another resource available in a simulation is Publication 17, *Your Federal Income Tax*. Although Publication 17, also referred to as Pub. 17, is available to you as a resource in the Regulation exam, it is *not* considered an authoritative source for research purposes. Pub. 17 is helpful if a candidate encounters a simulation that requires completion of a tax return. Pub. 17 contains the information and limits, such as standard deductions, personal exemption amounts, deduction limitations, and other information needed to complete a tax return.

As discussed in Chapter 1, Pub. 17 is a long document with over 250 pages of text. Knowledge of the contents and organization of Pub. 17 is important for the CPA Exam. If a candidate needs to access information quickly, there is not enough time during the CPA exam to browse through or read Pub. 17. However, if you are familiar with its organization and contents, Pub. 17 can be a useful tool for preparing an individual tax return.

Publication 17 is divided into six parts as shown in Exhibit 7.8.

**Exhibit 7.8: Publication 17, Your Federal Income Tax**

| Part | Topic |
|------|-------|
| One | The Income Tax Return |
| Two | Income |
| Three | Gains and Losses |
| Four | Adjustments to Income |
| Five | Standard Deduction and Itemized Deductions |
| Six | Figuring Your Taxes and Credits |

Notice the part numbers are entitled with spelled out numbers, such as one, two, and three. Each part is then divided into sections for certain topics and labeled with Arabic numbers, 1, 2, 3. However, these sections do not begin each section with 1, but continue on in the number. Exhibit 7.9 outlines the numbering system and the topics in Pub. 17.

**Exhibit 7-9: Publication 17, Your Federal Income Tax**

| Part | Number | Topic |
|------|--------|-------|
| **One** | | **The Income Tax Return** |
| | 1 | Filing Information |
| | 2 | Filing Status |
| | 3 | Personal Exemptions and Dependents |
| | 4 | Tax Withholding and Estimated Tax |
| **Two** | | **Income** |
| | 5 | Wages, Salaries, and Other Earnings |
| | 6 | Tip Income |
| | 7 | Interest Income |
| | 8 | Dividends and Other corporate Distributions |
| | 9 | Rental Income and Expenses |
| | 10 | Retirement Plans, Pensions, and Annuities |
| | 11 | Social Security and Equivalent Railroad Retirement Benefits |
| | 12 | Other Income |
| **Three** | | **Gains and Losses** |
| | 13 | Basis of Property |
| | 14 | Sale of Property |

| Part | Number | Topic |
|------|--------|-------|
|      | 15 | Selling Your Home |
|      | 16 | Reporting Gains and Losses |
| **Four** | | **Adjustments to Income** |
|      | 17 | Individual Retirement Arrangements |
|      | 18 | Alimony |
|      | 19 | Education-Related Adjustments |
| **Five** | | **Standard Deduction and Itemized Deductions** |
|      | 20 | Standard Deduction |
|      | 21 | Medical and Dental Expenses |
|      | 22 | Taxes |
|      | 23 | Interest Expense |
|      | 24 | Contributions |
|      | 25 | Nonbusiness Casualty and Theft Losses |
|      | 26 | Car Expenses and Other Employee Business Expense |
|      | 27 | Tax Benefits for Work-Related Education |
|      | 28 | Miscellaneous Deductions |
|      | 29 | Limit on Itemized Deductions |
| **Six** | | **Figuring Your Taxes and Credits** |
|      | 30 | How to Figure Your Tax |
|      | 31 | Tax on Investment Income of Certain Minor Children |
|      | 32 | Child and Dependent Care Credit |
|      | 33 | Credit for the Elderly or the Disabled |
|      | 34 | Child Tax Credit |
|      | 35 | Education Credits |
|      | 36 | Earned Income Credit |
|      | 37 | Other Credits |

Examine the table of contents in Exhibit 7.8 carefully. Notice that the order of Publication 17 is similar to the order of items completed on Form 1040. First is income, then other income, adjustments to income, deductions, and calculating taxes and credits. Tax tables are located in the back of Pub. 17.

It is highly recommended that you download a copy of Pub. 17. You can also receive a free copy at your local Internal Revenue Service office. Be sure to browse through this publication and familiarize yourself with its contents before the REG exam.

## STRATEGIES FOR RESEARCH IN REGULATION

If you know your way around the Internal Revenue Code, research on regulation might be your easiest section. Try to find your topic by opening up the table of contents and looking at the titles. If you cannot locate your topic in the table of contents, try a keyword search. If you believe you are close to the answer or in the correct section of the Code, you can perform a *search within* a particular area of the Code. Stay focused on how the Code is organized and you will have a better chance of finding your answer.

While you are studying technical content in tax, always focus your studying first on the normal rule, and then outline the exceptions to the rule. For example, if you know the exceptions to certain deduction rules for partnerships, you'll know when you need to look in the §700 series. The same study technique applies to corporations, S Corps, and personal holding companies. If you encounter an estate tax question, determine first whether it's an income issue or a transfer issue; then go to the appropriate part of the Code. Think first structurally, and then begin your search using the table of contents.

Your new quick study lists follow in Exhibits 7.10 and 7.11. Good luck with your tax research!

**Exhibit 7.10: Internal Revenue Code Subtitle A–Income Taxes Quick Study List**

| Subchapter | Topic | Section Numbers |
|:---:|:---|:---|
| A | Determination of Tax Liability | §1-59 |
| B | Computation of Taxable Income | §61-291 |
| C | Corporate Distributions and Adjustments | §300's |
| D | Deferred Compensation, etc. | §401-424 |
| E | Accounting Periods and Methods of Accounting | §441-483 |
| F | Exempt Organizations | §501-530 |
| G | Corporations Used to Avoid Income Tax on Shareholders | §531-565 |
| J | Estates, Trusts, Beneficiaries, and Decedents | §641-692 |
| K | Partners and Partnerships | §700's |
| N | Tax Based on Income from Sources within or without the United States | §861-999 |
| O | Gain or Loss on Disposition of Property | §1000's |
| P | Capital Gains and Losses | §1200's |
| Q | Readjustment of Tax between Years and Special Limitations | §1301-1351 |
| S | Tax Treatment of S Corporations and Their Shareholders | §1361-1379 |

**Exhibit 7.11:  Internal Revenue Code Subtitles B and F Quick Study List**

| Subtitle | Topic | Section Numbers |
|---|---|---|
| **B** | Estate and Gift Taxes | |
| Chapter 11 | Estate Tax | §2000, §2100, §2200 series |
| Chapter 12 | Gift Tax | §2500 series |
| Chapter 13 | Tax on Generation-Skipping Transfers | §2600 series |
| Chapter 14 | Special Valuation Rules | §2700 series |
| **F** | Procedure and Administration | §6000 and §7000 series |

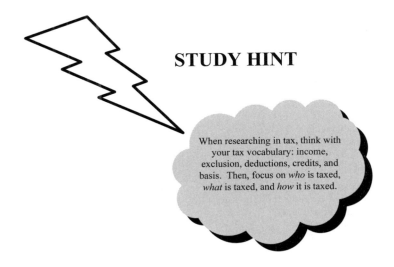

**STUDY HINT**

When researching in tax, think with your tax vocabulary: income, exclusion, deductions, credits, and basis.  Then, focus on *who* is taxed, *what* is taxed, and *how* it is taxed.

## TEST YOURSELF

**1.** The highest level of organization of the tax code is
    a.    Subchapters.
    b.    Subparagraphs.
    c.    Subtitles.
    d.    Sections.

**2.** Which of the following is a proper designation for a subchapter?
    a.    Subchapter C.
    b.    Subchapter 1.
    c.    Subchapter IV.
    d.    Subchapter (f).

**3.** In tax research, what part of the code is cited in the answer?
    a.    Chapter number.
    b.    Subtitle number.
    c.    Clause number.
    d.    Section number.

**4.** In what part of the Internal Revenue Code will you find the rules for partners and partnerships?
    a.    Subchapter B.
    b.    Subchapter C.
    c.    Subchapter K.
    d.    Subchapter S.

**5.** In what part of the Internal Revenue Code will you find the rules for corporate distributions and adjustments?
    a.    Subchapter B.
    b.    Subchapter C.
    c.    Subchapter K.
    d.    Subchapter S.

**6.** In what part of the Internal Revenue Code will you find the rules for S Corporations?
    a.    Subchapter B.
    b.    Subchapter C.
    c.    Subchapter K.
    d.    Subchapter S.

**7.** Which sections of the Internal Revenue Code will have the rules for partnerships?
    a.    Sections 61-291.
    b.    Sections 501-530.
    c.    Section 701 through 799.
    d.    Sections 1201 through 1299.

**8.** Which sections of the Internal Revenue Code will have the rules for determining tax liability?
    a.    Sections 1-59.
    a.    Sections 61-291.
    b.    Sections 501-530.
    d.    Sections 1201 through 1299.

**9.** Which sections of the Internal Revenue Code will have the rules for computation of taxable income?
    a.    Sections 61-291.
    b.    Sections 501-530.
    c.    Section 701 through 799.
    d.    Sections 1201 through 1299.

**10.** Which sections of the Internal Revenue Code will have the rules for gain or loss on disposition of property?
    a.    Sections 61-291.
    b.    Sections 501-530.
    c.    Section 701 through 799.
    d.    Sections 1201 through 1299.

## PRACTICE YOUR RESEARCH SKILLS

1. Timothy Swift receives dividends from an investment in XYZ Corporation. Should the dividends be included in income on his federal income tax return?

2. Tom Hancock receives interest on a registered local municipal bond. Should the interest be included as income in his federal income tax return?

3. Can a partnership deduct charitable contributions on its Form 1065 partnership tax return?

4. Colfax Corporation estimates bad debt expense on its accrual basis income statement of $1,000. During the year, an $800 account receivable is determined to be worthless. What amount should Colfax deduct on the federal tax return for the bad debt?

5. Storm Corporation was fined $10,000 for violating Environmental Protection Regulations. Can Storm Corporation deduct this amount on their federal income tax return?

6. Landau has a net operating loss in 2008. What are the limits as to how many years the loss can be carried back or carried forward?

7. How is the basis of a partner in a partnership calculated?

8. What is the maximum number of shareholders that can exist in an S Corporation?

9. Sheryl Patton, an individual taxpayer who is single, has a capital loss of $20,000 during the year. Sheryl also has a capital gain of $5,000 during the year. What amount can Sheryl deduct as a capital loss on her federal income tax return?

10. Huffman Corporation, a C Corporation, has taxable income of $180,000. At what tax rate will Huffman Corporation be taxed for federal income tax purposes?

# 8 UNDERSTANDING SEARCH ENGINES

Search engines are fascinating and powerful tools for research. I have spent hundreds of hours using various versions of the infobases in financial accounting, auditing, and taxation. As a master's student in taxation and as a practitioner, I have researched in the hard copy tax literature. As a faculty member, I have taught research in financial accounting and auditing when the infobases were originally in a DOS-based format. I have written infobase instructions for students in my classes. I have coauthored an applied professional research text. I have also worked with both the CD versions and online versions of the infobases. In other words, I have been immersed in the infobases long enough to notice the similarities and differences with each infobase.

Of course, each program has its own strengths and weaknesses. Our goal is to make you aware of the strengths of each infobase, avoid the weaknesses of each infobase, and get you up to speed fast on research. Let's start with an overview to search engines and infobases.

## UNDERSTANDING INFOBASES AND SEARCH ENGINES

First, it is important to understand how various infobases work. Not all infobases are programmed alike! Understanding the differences will help you determine which search strategies work best with each infobase.

An infobase is a collection of information. The information is divided into parts. Some programs call these *records*, other programs refer to them as *documents*. These records or documents are available for searching, and the results are listed in some organized fashion.

The FARS CD, AICPA Resource CD, AICPA onLine Publications, FARS Online, and the CPA exam all use slightly different search engines, different search menus, and different algorithms for producing search results. Understanding these differences will help you understand how each particular infobase functions. It will also help you transfer your research skills from one infobase to another.

First, if you normally use the FARS CD or AICPA Resource CD, these CD infobases use a search engine that is considerably different from the online versions of the infobases. FARS CD and AICPA Resource CD searches, selects, and displays the research results differently from AICPA onLine Publications, FARS Online, or the CPA sample exam interface.

The FARS CD and AICPA Resource use a Folio interface and search engine. Personally, I love Folio. I think it is one of the finest pieces of programming I have ever used. The interface looks a little different on the FARS CD than it does on AICPA Resource, but the search engine operates almost the same for these two infobases. Actually, the FARS CD interface is slightly more user friendly.

## FOLIO VIEWS

Folio Views is a program developed by NextPage, Inc. NextPage specializes in creating infobases from hard copy works such as the accounting pronouncements or the auditing standards. We will use the FASB's authoritative literature in our discussion of Folio Views. From now on, we will refer to it simply as Folio with a capital letter.

Folio contains an advanced search command that requires the user to type in the Boolean operators. The researcher is responsible for developing a search with the correct syntax. When you open the program, you can select the contents tab and drill down through the table of contents menus. You can also remain in the document window and perform a keyword search.

Understanding how Folio organizes information is important. This is an important distinction: Folio divides the standards into "records." In Folio, a record can be a title, a subtitle, or a paragraph. Usually a record is a paragraph. When you search for a word, it finds all of the records, usually paragraphs, where that term is found.

In Folio, when you search for an item with the advanced search command, it does not use any algorithms to prioritize results. Folio does not do anything fancy to the results—it gives you *exactly* what you queried. More importantly, Folio displays the results *exactly* in the same order as the records are found in the infobase. Therefore, if the infobase is in chronological order, such as FARS, the matching records or "hits" are displayed in precisely this order. This is extremely helpful for learning your way around the standards because results are always given in the same order: the ARBs, the APBs, and the FAS.

Folio displays all records where the term is found. Since this is a character string search, and *not* a topical search, it searches for exactly what you typed. If you can't spell, you won't get any matches. If you do not hyphenate correctly, you may not find your answer. In the advanced search window, you can monitor the number of hits as you type in your keywords or search string. In addition, in the advanced search command, you also have access to a word window that displays all words and derivations of words in the infobase. This word window is especially helpful if you have spelling problems.

If you want a derivation of a word, then you must use the correct word or the correct Boolean operators to retrieve those results. The results in Folio are *exactly* what you asked for, and they are *always* in the same order as the infobase, (i.e. ARBs first, then APBs, then FASB Statements).

In Folio, the results window groups together and displays all of the records where the search term was found. These results are displayed in their entirety. If your search produced 643 results, when you click on the documents tab for the results, you will retrieve all 643 paragraphs and can scroll through the results. You do not have a results list here. You have the actual results in the window, paragraph by paragraph. The results document show the hits or matches highlighted in blue. You can use your arrow keys to move from highlighted word to highlighted word, or from record to record.

In Folio, if you want a results list showing where the hits are located, you can look at the "Contents" pane or tab. The contents tab displays an expandable list that indicates how many hits are located within each pronouncement. (See Appendix B to learn how to reset the menu options to do this.) In the contents list, the titles of the pronouncements are clearly listed, as well as the number of hits in each standard.   You can continue to expand the contents list within the standard to find exactly where each hit is located.

If you want to read the entire standard, you can choose that particular standard from the contents list by clicking on the standard. The standard is retrieved in its entirety, and you can read the standard from beginning to end. If you only want to read the relevant paragraph, you can click on that standard in the contents list, and use your arrow keys to locate each hit within that standard.

With Folio, when you select "History," it gives you the history of all the keyword searches you have performed, and you can move or toggle between these searches. When you hit the Back button, it goes backwards into the previous search. You can also go Forward and move between searches. If you continue to go Back, you will back completely out of your search into the main menu.

Once you know how to use Folio, it doesn't matter what kind of Folio infobase you are searching; the infobases essentially work the same. See Appendix B for more hints on using the FARS CD-ROM with the Folio interface. If you change a few of the default settings, you will find it's easier and much more fun to use!

### OTHER SEARCH ENGINES

Now let's look at other search engines and how they function. This is the interesting part. The FARS Online infobase, AICPA onLine Publications, and the CPA exam use a completely different interface and search engine than those used by Folio-based products. Again, NextPage develops some of these other search engines. These other search engines are similar to an internet search. FARS Online, AICPA onLine, and the CPA sample exam use a search engine that is similar to an Internet search.

These two types of search engines (Folio CD products and Online search products) are programmed very differently. First, the manner in which the information is divided is different. For example, the FARS CD divides the infobase into records, which is usually a paragraph. FARS Online does not divide the infobase into records or paragraphs, but into documents. This is a super important distinction! A "document" is a set of paragraphs delineated by some heading in the literature or by a break that the programmer places in the literature. If you look closely at FARS Online, some documents may be one paragraph, others three paragraphs, and others 10-12 paragraphs. This means that when you use a keyword search and retrieve a document, you are retrieving much more than just the paragraph in which the keyword is found.

Second, if you are searching for two terms, such as depreciation and asset, this search engine gives you the results where both terms are found in the same *document*. The terms are not necessarily located in the same paragraph. This can be problematic because in the online product, the "and" operator will expand the search much differently from the CD product. The Online version may produce considerably more information in your results. This causes the researcher to read more documents to find the answer.

Third, the way the search engines operate and display results is also very different. Recall that the CD version produced results in chronological order. These Internet-type search engines use algorithms to prioritize results. This is another *super* important distinction. The search results are not displayed in the same order as the infobase. Instead, the results will be jumbled up in what appears to the researcher as a random order.

Fourth, the results are displayed in a list of document titles. "Results" is a list of results, not the actual paragraphs. You must click on each listing to view the actual documents with the hits. It can be much more time-consuming to click on each result to view the document and determine if it is on point.

## A SEARCH EXAMPLE

Let's walk through a search using the FARS CD product, and then replicate that search with FARS Online. We will search for the terms *depreciable asset*.

### Using the FARS CD to Search

Using the June 2007 version FARS CD, I clicked on the large pair of binoculars in the toolbar to start an advanced search. When the word *depreciable* is typed, the search results window indicates there are 89 matches for the word depreciable. When I type in the word asset, there are 2881 matches. The results window also shows that the number of records or paragraphs where the two words are found together is 38. After clicking on enter or *ok*, the 38 paragraphs are retrieved.  Note that you must be in the documents window to scroll through or use the arrow keys to click through the paragraphs retrieved.

If you would like a listing of the citations where these results are found, merely click on the contents tab, and expand the table by clicking on the plus signs.  Now you can see the title of every pronouncement where the terms *depreciable asset* are found together in the same paragraph.  Analyzing the titles of the pronouncement is a very fast and efficient way to determine if any of the retrieved paragraphs are on point.

**Using FARS Online**

Now, let's walk through that same example with FARS Online.  When you search for keywords, remember FARS Online finds all documents where the word or words are found. There are two ways to search:  simple search and advanced search.  Depending on whether you are using a simple search or an advanced search, the program displays the results in a completely different manner.

In a simple search, the results appear to be in chronological order, or in the same order the items are found in the infobase.  However, in the advanced search, the program prioritizes the results by some algorithm.  This is not exactly good for accounting research, because it does *not* prioritize the documents by hierarchy or category of GAAP, but it prioritizes them by some language selection criteria.

To begin, let's use a simple search for *depreciable asset* in FARS Online.  There are 106 results.  Notice that this is a significantly higher number of results than we found with the FARS CD product.  In other words, the FARS Online version will increase the number of matches because it retrieves all documents where both words are found anywhere within the same document.  The FARS CD, on the other hand, retrieves only the paragraphs where both words are found in the same paragraph.

With FARS Online, the results of a *simple* search were displayed in somewhat of a chronological order of pronouncements, (i.e. ARB, then APB, then FASB Statements, with all Current Text citations after that, and then EITF Abstracts, and FASB Implementation Guides after that).  Essentially, the results were in the same order as the literature.  That's good.

Let's search again using FARS Online with an advanced search for *depreciable asset.*  Again, there are 106 results, which is significantly more material to read than the results produced by the FARS CD product.

Now let's compare our FARS Online results of the advanced search with the Online version of the simple search.  Notice that the advanced search results are not listed in the same order as the simple search results.  In fact, the advanced results list did not appear to be in any order of importance of GAAP or hierarchy of GAAP.  The Implementation Guides were first, followed by Appendices from FAS 96 (which, by the way, is completely superseded), and then Appendices from FAS 109. As you look at these results, you may be thinking, "What is this mess?"

Evidently, the Online program counts the number of times the word is in the document. The program prioritizes documents with more keyword matches as more important results. It then displays the results in this prioritized order. Think about this method and how it relates to accounting research. This method can produce some very unhelpful results in accounting research.

In the accounting standards, the rule is stated very succinctly. There will be two or three sentences in the standard that define the rule. The appendices, introduction, and summary, and dissenting opinions have more verbose language—these aren't the rules, and we don't cite those.

Again, these Internet-type search engines are programmed to count the number of times the word is found in the "document" and prioritize the document as more important. That's why you might see the Q&A, appendices, summary, introduction, or dissenting opinions listed as top priority in your research results. Again, these prioritization rules have nothing to do with GAAP or the hierarchy of GAAP. These longer passages containing more matches are *not* the rules, and we don't usually cite them when doing research.

FARS Online, AICPA onLine Publications, and the CPA sample exam search engines all use an algorithm or statistical approach to finding and prioritizing search results. The CPA sample exam allows Natural Language Searching, which searches for word forms and produces statistically relevant results. These results are based on how frequently the query term appears in a document, the document length, and the completeness. It prioritizes the results in some order derived by that algorithm. Therefore, you will get results based on how often the word is used in a particular "document."

I have also analyzed some of the "documents" on the sample exam. I have compared these documents to the hard copy (paper) version of the standards. From what I can determine by clicking around on the few pronouncements that are available in the sample exam infobase, it appears the programmer created a new document whenever there was a bold heading. The difficult part is that the document was given the title of the bold heading. Therefore, the search results show the bold heading, rather than the pronouncement number and bold heading. That is why you will see results with a vague title like Statement 1 or Section B.

The commercial version of FARS Online displays results slightly different from the CPA sample exam. Although the commercial version of the database also jumbles the order of results, it lists the complete citation in front of each result. Having a full citation is helpful for knowing whether you are in older standards or newer standards, or whether you are in an appendix or dissenting opinion.

## COMPARING FARS ONLINE WITH THE CPA EXAM

As you will see in our next chapter, the CPA exam search engine produces results that look similar to an Internet search. That's why it takes practice and knowledge of the standards so you don't waste time reading appendices, introductions, summaries, dissenting opinions, or other areas where the accounting rules are not located.

Once we know how the CPA sample exam infobase works, you can develop a research strategy that will work for you on the exam. Let's look at the CPA sample exam interface more in depth in Chapter 9.

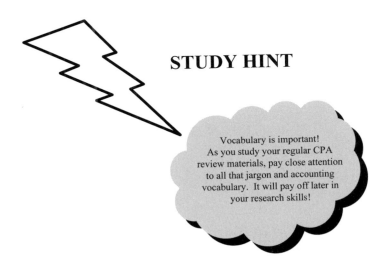

## STUDY HINT

Vocabulary is important!
As you study your regular CPA
review materials, pay close attention
to all that jargon and accounting
vocabulary. It will pay off later in
your research skills!

# 9 GETTING READY FOR THE EXAM

## THE RESEARCH INTERFACE

By now, you've realized that there is one important factor you need to pass the CPA exam: *Knowledge*. But there is also a second very important factor in passing: *Confidence*.

Confidence in your technical knowledge and research skills will lower your test anxiety. A lower test anxiety means you will think more clearly on the exam. Lower test anxiety also means you will manage your time better on the exam.

The most important way to build confidence to pass the CPA exam is by knowing your material well and by being familiar with the exam interface. Time is critical on the CPA exam; therefore, you need to be proficient with the interface to avoid time loss. You must be comfortable with the format for answering different types of questions. You must be comfortable with using the CPA exam interface for spreadsheets, formulas, and the calculator, as well as the software program for the professional research literature.

## THE CPA EXAM INTERFACE

I have spent literally *hours* clicking on every button on each of the sample exams. I usually have two computers running side-by-side; the sample exam on one machine and Microsoft Word on the other machine. I intentionally enter nonsensical data and make wrong entries so I can see how the program reacts. I take notes as I point and click. I screen-capture certain pages and analyze the exam questions and the exam interface.

After spending hours with the sample exams in FAR, AUD, REG and BEC, I have learned some very important things: Although the exam interface is fairly intuitive, it has some features that take a little more time to master. It also has some features that are unique and not so intuitive. And it has other features that are relatively frustrating.

Silly little things, such as: Do you click or double click? How do you enter numbers in the answer spaces? How do you add or multiply with the calculator? How do you use the spreadsheets? How do you search on the infobases? How do you open up the table of contents wider so you can read the titles in the standards? How do you highlight answers for research? How do you cut and paste? Even if you lose 15 seconds here and there, the lost time adds up to possibly running out of time on the exam.

In this chapter, we will focus on understanding the search engine and learning how to use the research interface on the CPA exam. We will also discuss search strategies for the research components on the CPA exam. There are also some tips on what to watch out for with the exam interface in general. In Appendix D, there are additional tips on other parts of the interface of the CPA Exam.

## THE INFOBASE ON THE CPA EXAM

Now let's concentrate on the CPA sample exam. The CPA sample exam search engine appears to be a simplified version of the FARS Online search engine. There are two search functions on the CPA exam: simple search and advanced search. You should be aware that they can produce considerably different results. Therefore, you should practice extensively with each search command until you master them and can determine which search command works best for you.

If you use the search function immediately upon entering the infobase, you will see results from all three sources: the Original Pronouncements as Amended, the Current Text, and the Topical Index. This gives you a great deal of information to read if you try to search all areas of the infobase at once. Actually, searching all three areas provides too much information most of the time.

If you click on Original Pronouncements, and then type in a keyword, and click on *Within*, this will keep your search within the Original Pronouncements as Amended. Searching within will limit the number of matches. The *Search Within* command on the CPA exam is similar to the *Search Within* command in the FARS Online search engine.

After you enter your search terms, you need to view the results of your search. The *View Results* command allows you to view the list of results. Sometimes, the results list is not very helpful because the titles are not descriptive as to the source of the document. In order to see the source or citation for the pronouncement being retrieved, you must open the document. When you open the document, the source is listed in bold black print at the top of the document. To read the document, scroll through the document. To go back to the list of results, click *View Results*. The list of results window reappears, and you can select another result to read. Viewing results of keyword searches can be a time-consuming process. If you intend to search by keywords, practice moving back and forth between the results list and the documents so you become faster.

Once you open a document in the results list, the title changes to a different color in your view results list. If you open a document, the title in the list turns maroon. If the document has not been opened, it remains blue. This, of course, is similar to an internet search. This is a nice feature of the program because you can see which results you have read.

Other important functions on the CPA exam interface are *Back*, *View History*, *Clear*, and *Home*. Exhibit 9.1 outlines a brief description of the most important functions.

**Exhibit 9.1: CPA Sample Exam Research Interface**

| Button | Description |
|---|---|
| Back | You can go back, but you can't go forward. Also, back takes you to the last previous screen you viewed, not the last search. |
| View history | Contains the last 20 pages that you viewed. It does NOT give you the history of your search terms. |
| Home | Takes you back to the front of the infobase in the table of contents, so you can start over. However, you do not have a fresh start because the program keeps all of the history from that portion of the exam. |
| Clear | This command is hidden in the Advanced Search. Don't forget to clear the advanced search if you need to start over. |
| View results | This gives you a list of results from your search. Sometimes the titles aren't very descriptive or linked back to the exact location in the infobase. |
| Advanced | Advanced shows Boolean operator choices. Watch out for stemming. Check the box for searching within level when appropriate. |
| Within | This is powerful for narrowing the search. Within searches within a particular level or folder that you select. |

## THE SIMPLE SEARCH

Let's explore the simple search further. The search command on the CPA sample exam interface is a simple search. At first, I thought that this simple search might produce results that were in chronological order or in the same order of the standards. However, after working with it over several days trying out many searches, the program still seems to prioritize the results by some algorithm, rather than listing them in a specific order.

A nice feature of the simple search is the ability to search within a particular standard. You can search within a particular area or level of the infobase (i.e., Original Pronouncements, ARBs, APB, or FASB Statements), by clicking on the appropriate folder, typing in your search terms, and then clicking on *Within*. This narrows your search nicely. Search within is particularly fast when you know your accounting pronouncement, and click on the relevant part that should have the accounting rules. This is very fast with the FASB Standards. Try it with the one of the standards on the sample exam.

One peculiarity with the CPA exam infobase is caused by the way the infobase is divided into documents. When you search for two terms, if you do not use quotes, it will search for documents where both terms are found in the document—not where they are found in the same paragraph or where the words are found together. This produces results that may be completely irrelevant. Search within can sometimes help alleviate this problem by focusing on the appropriate standard. Of course, you need to know your way around the standards to search within a particular standard.

Another method for counteracting the irrelevant results produced in keyword searches is to use quotes around your search terms in the simple search. This very quickly narrows the search. The only problem with this strategy is that you must have a very precise accounting vocabulary to find the answer. For example, you would need to know whether the standard uses the terms *depreciable asset, assets to be depreciated,* or *depreciation of assets.* You will see very different results with each of these search terms!

## THE ADVANCED SEARCH

Now we will examine the advanced search more in depth. The advanced search has several search choices. They are

- Containing **all** of these words
- **Not** containing any of these words
- Containing **one or more** of these words
- Containing this **exact phrase**
- Containing these words **near** each other

Let's talk about each of these searches. Exhibit 9.2 outlines each search feature.

**Exhibit 9.2: Search Feature**

| CPA Sample Exam | Explanation | FARS CD-ROM Equivalent |
|---|---|---|
| Containing **all** of these words | Defaults to AND operator | & |
| **Not** containing any of these words | NOT operator | ^ |
| Containing **one or more** of these words | EITHER OR operator | \| |
| Containing this **exact phrase** | Quotations marks | "xxx" |
| Containing these words **near** each other | Proximity search | Ordered proximity  /<br>Unordered proximity  @ |

At the bottom of these choices, you have more choices where you can check the box for these items.

- Find alternate word forms (stemming)
- Find synonyms (thesaurus)
- Search within the currently selected text

Again, we can equate these to other search engines as shown in Exhibit 9.3.

**Exhibit 9.3: Search Engines**

| AICPA Sample Exam | Explanation | FARS CD-ROM Equivalent |
|---|---|---|
| Find alternate word forms | Wildcard | * |
| Find synonyms | Thesaurus | Just don't go here!!!! |
| Search within | Searches only within selected document | [ ] |

As we discussed earlier, if you are searching all areas of the infobase, you will probably have too many results to manage. *Search Within* is probably the best and most powerful option because it narrows the search.

You will also see other search commands such as finding synonyms with the thesaurus. Don't go there! This feature does not look for accounting terminology; it is just a regular thesaurus. If you are trying to use that command during the exam, you have reached a point of desperation, and you should not waste any more time. Remember, you should *not* be trying out new things during the exam. You must practice searching before the exam, and you must rely on the research methods that are within your comfort zone.

You can use the advanced search to narrow your search. However, beware—the advanced search also produces results in a different order of priority. Advanced search prioritizes results based on the program's algorithms. The advanced search results will not be displayed in the same order as the simple search results. With advanced search, the number of matches, the results, and the order of the results can be very different. You should practice with advanced search on the sample exam before relying on it during the real exam.

Three other features are found in the advanced search: Stemming (alternate word forms), thesaurus, and search within the currently selected text. Stemming will broaden your search. Stemming is not necessarily a good feature when you are under time pressure because it produces *more* results to read. In my version of the FAR sample exam, the stemming box was automatically checked. Watch out for this, and don't let the infobase give you too many results that you don't want. If stemming is already checked as a default setting and you don't want it, be sure to uncheck this box.

The thesaurus is often inappropriate for accounting research. The thesaurus is only a regular thesaurus, and it is not unique or modified to our accounting jargon. Therefore, the thesaurus will produce some very strange results. I typed in *debt* on the sample exam and was sent on a wild reading adventure! I found hits for items charged against earnings, documents with the word *debit*, documents with the words *deferred, assess,* and *shares for ESOPs*. None of these terms were relevant to debt. Yes, it did give me a few hits on topics related to liabilities, but the thesaurus produced far too many irrelevant results. Stay away from the thesaurus completely. It is not time well spent when you are studying for the exam, practicing with the sample exam, or working the CPA exam. It is a time sink you do *not* want to fall into!

So, it appears that the search command on the screen is a "simple" search and will give you results in some prioritized order. This is nice. However, the search results do not give you titles that are referenced to the exact pronouncement. That's bad. Let's explore this further with an example.

## A SEARCH EXAMPLE

To help you understand the sample exam interface, let's walk through a search and analyze our results. If you open the standards on the FAR sample exam and search for *depreciation*, most of your results are matches to the topical index. It also gives you a few matches from the Original Pronouncements and the Current Text. These results are not very helpful.

If you click on Original Pronouncements as Amended, search for *depreciation* and click on *Within*, this will narrow the search for equipment to the Original Pronouncements as Amended. Notice that now your search results are limited to the documents from the Original Pronouncements as Amended. But look more closely at this list. The titles are very cryptic. These titles are not helpful in finding anything. Section B. Section B of what? Where did *Criteria for Extraordinary Items* come from? Appraisal of Alternative Procedures? Present Accounting? Statement 3? Section A? Section B? Section C? These titles do not help you understand where the results are in the infobase. You would have to click on every one of these titles and read it to determine the source—which is *very* time-consuming.

In the top right-hand corner of your results window, there is a selection marked *View*. I changed my view to short, medium, and long, and I did not find that feature very helpful. For me, the short, medium, and long titles cluttered up my screen and were distracting. You may find that you like this feature. However, you should extensively practice with it to determine if it saves you time or costs you time in completing your research. Again, the only way to determine the source or citation for many of the results was to click on the result and read the bold black print at the top of the retrieved document, which is time-consuming.

The lack of citations and the jumbled organization of results make the search function on the CPA exam infobase somewhat challenging to use. That's why it is so important to be familiar with the standards. If you are familiar with the standards, using the table of contents menu on the left, and dropping the titles down may be more helpful and faster.

It also helps to resize the table of contents window. To resize the window, click and drag the divider to the right. Now you can easily read the titles. You're ready to dig down into the table of contents to find your answer.

The table of contents feature in the CPA exam infobase is quite helpful. It also outlines how the programmers divided up the infobase into "documents." If there is a file folder symbol, this means you can open that topic further and look at a specific area under that topic.

In order to understand our search results, we need to talk more about documents. To me, a document is a full paper document or standard, such as ARB 43, or APB 18, or FAS 5. However, that is not how the programmers defined a document in the CPA exam infobase. To the programmer, a document is just a defined area of the text. When you look at the delineations for documents that the programmers made in the standards, it appears they placed a field marker and started a new document on most of the bolded headings. I compared the CPA infobase "documents" to my hard copy version of the pronouncements. Although not always the case, beginning a new document at every bold heading appears to be the manner in which the infobase was organized.

When you analyze the results in our search for depreciation, you will find that not all paragraphs contain the search term. However, each document should have at least one paragraph with the search term highlighted.

## USING THE TABLE OF CONTENTS

You can use the table of contents to your advantage if you know your way around the infobase. First, remember that the ARBs are divided into chapters. All the chapters are clearly outlined in the table of contents. Drag your table of contents window *wide* open so you can read all of the chapter titles. This helps a great deal in the search. If you find something relevant, you can do a search *within* that particular document. Using the table of contents and searching allows you to research a topic quickly.

Remember our friends, the little APBs? Open up one of the APBs on the CPA sample exam. You will see folders for summary, background, opinion, etc. After studying the organization and structure of the pronouncements, you know that the accounting rules are in the Opinion paragraph. When you find your topic, find the opinion folder and do a search *within*.

This same principle works with the FASB Statements. Open a FASB Statement in the Original Pronouncements. In the 2007 version of the sample exam, FAS 130 was included in the infobase. Again, the beauty of the table of contents is that when you enter FAS 130, you know the rules are not in the introduction or summary. You can skip this. You should not be wasting time reading the introduction or summary. Bypass it! What you need are the accounting *standards.* Click on that, and you should see about ten documents. The titles for these "documents" follow the boldfaced nonitalicized headings in FAS 130 for all of the accounting rules. Practice this, and you will see how easy it is to click down through the table of contents of the standards folder and find the topic needed.

## SEARCH STRATEGIES

### Original Pronouncements or Current Text?

Deciding whether to use the Original Pronouncements or the Current Text is a personal choice. These two resources are definitely organized differently. The Current Text contains a summary in front of each topic. On the CPA exam, it appears that the summary cannot be selected and transferred to answer. Items that can be selected as the answer include the paragraphs with rules and disclosures, as well as the glossary and definitions near the end of each section.

One important point to realize is that searching the Original Pronouncements and the Current Text simultaneously produces far too many results to handle. You might choose just one, either the Original Pronouncement or the Current Text, and search within to determine which produces better and faster research results.

Personally, I prefer the Original Pronouncements because I know my way around them. For me, the Current Text is more time-consuming because this edited version of the literature is in the order designed by the Current Text authors. Sometimes I use the topical index or the current text when I want to look at some different keywords. Again, this is a personal choice that you must make based on your knowledge and experience with the standards. Be sure to practice extensively with both sources to determine which resource works best for you!

### My Search Strategies

I have different research strategies depending on which version of the infobase I am using. When I am researching with the FARS CD product, I always use keyword searches and the contents window. But when I am using the CPA sample exam, I completely change my approach.

After spending quite a few hours on the CPA sample exam infobase, I find my best strategy is to go straight to the pronouncement if I know which pronouncement should have the answer. I open the table of contents window very wide by dragging the window divider open. I click on the pronouncement. Then I add a search within that particular document. I type in my search string, and click *Within*, and search within that document or area of the infobase.

Searching within is great. If I know the answer should be in the ARBs (really old material), I go straight to the ARB area of the infobase. If I remember the topic is in the APB study list, I go to the APBs and look for the Opinion paragraphs. If the topic was addressed in the earlier FASB Statements, I can look through the list of standards to find the topic. Using the infobase in the order of the standards is much easier for me than using a keyword search and trying to read through a jumbled list of results. I find using a keyword search and prioritized list of results more time-consuming and difficult to use than using information that is in the chronological order of the standards.

## Developing YOUR Search Strategies

Many CPA candidates believe they can rely on the advanced search engine and not know their way around the infobase. They think, "I can search in the infobase; I can just look it up." This is not necessarily true.

Although the content of the exam is not to be disclosed, many candidates discuss their overall exam experience. I have heard some sad stories. When I ask students how research went, some say, "Oh, I got lucky—I found my question right away." Others say, "I spent 30 minutes sifting through the jumbled results of keyword searches, and I had to give up." Others say they spent too much time on research in the simulations and ran out of time on the exam. Keep in mind, keyword searches will only find the information if you have a *precise* accounting vocabulary. And that precision must match how the ARB, APB, or FASB worded it when the standard was issued.

The most important advice I can give you when using these search functions is this: *Watch your time!* It is easy to lose precious time on this exam by getting bogged down in a search. Watch your time. Know when to cut your losses and move on!

As we say in accounting: What's the bottom line? Keyword searches are great if you have a lot of time. If not, your best strategy is to actually know your way around the standards. Remember, there is no substitute for knowledge!

With your knowledge of the standards and your knowledge of the navigation and search techniques available on the CPA exam infobase, you are now ready to practice and find *your* best strategy for research on the CPA exam. Again, practice until you feel comfortable. You will find what works best and fastest for you!

## THE SIMULATION INTERFACE

Now let's talk a little more about the exam interface. We'll look at how the simulation interfaces are similar in FAR, AUD, and REG.

In the simulations, you have two types of tabs here. Some tabs are *information* tabs, and other tabs are *work* tabs. The information tabs normally begin on the left with directions, situation, standards, and resources. In various parts of the exam (i.e., FAR, AUD, and REG), the tabs might be labeled differently (i.e., Standards or Code).  The tab area is where the standards for research are located.

There is another tab called *Resources*.  This is strange, because you would think that the infobase is a resource, especially since the AICPA calls its infobase AICPA Resource.  However, that's not the case.  On the CPA exam, under Resources, you will find resources such as spreadsheet operators, spreadsheet functions, analytical formulas, or MACRS tables.  The contents of Resources depend on which section of the exam you are taking.  Do *not* assume that the same resources are identical for each section of the exam.  Also, do *not* assume that you have access to any of these resources during the multiple-choice components of the exam.

For example, in AUD, the definitions for formulas such as current ratio, times interest earned, etc. are in Resources.  However, knowledge of these ratios may also be tested in FAR or BEC, but you may not be given the formula table in resources. That is why it is important to check the sample exam for *each* section of the CPA exam before you sit for that particular section.

Also, no resources are available during the multiple-choice portion of the exam.  You only have access to the online calculator with basic functions of add, subtract, multiply, divide, and square root.  When you're in the multiple-choice section, you are on your own.   You do not have any infobases to consult, and no formulas to help you with answers.  Therefore, you must rely on your knowledge.

Another important point to make is that in Version 1.5 of the CPA exam interface, the AICPA made some excellent improvements.  This is important if you have previously taken the exam with the original interface (pre-April 2006).  If you took any part of the exam with Version 1.0, make *sure* you practice with this latest sample exam interface.  Do *not* assume that the infobases and research commands work the same as in Version 1.0.

In the Version 1.5 interface, there are two different split screen options: vertical and horizontal.  Another interesting change is that the Standards button is now in the work tab area.  (Formerly, it was in the upper right-hand boxes.)  Watch out!  On some simulations, particularly in AUD, you may have too many tabs to fit onto the screen.  Therefore, some work tabs may go off to the right of the screen, and you must cursor over to get them out and work them.  In other words, all the work tabs may not be showing.  Make sure you check that you have completed all work tabs by scrolling to the right on the simulation.  You do not want to accidentally miss completing a part of a simulation.

Another important point is that once you do *anything* in a particular work tab, the tab becomes shaded.  Even though you may not have completely finished all the parts of that tab, the tab still changes shade.  Therefore, you may think you are finished with that part of the simulation. Not true! If you skip parts, you won't remember what you skipped and what you have to go back and finish. You may lose valuable time on the exam trying to go back and finish up loose ends. My advice is to work clean, work neat, work it in the order given, and *move on*!

## Transferring Your Answers in Research

If you know your way around the standards, you can use the table of contents to find your answer. You can keep drilling down and expanding the folders until you see your topic in the selection. This is where it comes in handy to know what is old and what is new—what's in the ARBs, the APBs, and the FASB Statements.

A word of caution here: The instructions tell you to split your screen. Splitting the screen makes research difficult because it limits the amount of material you can read in the search. When I split my screen, I counted nine lines of infobase text on the sample exam on my computer. If you cannot read the material, and you constantly have to scroll, the search becomes very cumbersome and difficult. I find working with a smaller view frustrating.

However, there is a very important point to make. Beware!!

**When researching, the screen *must* be split in order to highlight or transfer your answer. You cannot even *highlight* the answer when you find it unless the screen is split.**

Before you attempt to highlight an answer, you must open the *Research* tab, split the screen, and open the *Standards* tab. You must be in both the *Standards* and the *Research* tabs to highlight an answer. Make sure you are actually on the *Research* tab after you split the screen. Sometimes when I split the screen, the sample exam sends me back to the first instruction tab, and I don't realize that I am no longer in the *Research* tab. I figured this out when I tried to highlight an answer and the little symbol would not go away. You need to be in the *Research* tab *and* the *Standards* tab.

Don't forget to split your screen. I have played with the sample exam for *hours* and I could not get the exam to highlight or transfer the answer. I kept getting that ⊘ symbol. Again, the instructions tell you that if the symbol is shown, you cannot transfer that to an answer. The instructions also tell you that the symbol indicates an incorrect answer that cannot be highlighted or transferred. Any correct answer will allow you to highlight it. Therefore, when I kept getting that little symbol, I thought, "Hmm, that must not be the answer." At one point, I said, "I *know* this is the correct answer. Why won't this answer highlight?" The symbol will *not* change or allow the text to be highlighted as an answer until you *split your screen.* Don't forget this.

Of course, the directions on the sample exam tell you to split your screen. Unfortunately, when you read these directions quickly, you do not realize the importance of this simple instruction. That is why it is important to actually work with the sample exam, so that you are absolutely *sure* you understand all instructions and all functions of the exam interface.

It is sad, but I have had reports from candidates who could not get the research answer to transfer in their exam. They said they *knew* they had the right answer for the research, but they couldn't get it to transfer. I am wondering now if it is because their screen was not split.

The AICPA has addressed this issue by placing a special notice about exam functionality on their Web page. Be sure to check the AICPA Web page prior to taking the exam, and look for any updates or changes on exam functionality. Also, be sure to practice with this on the sample exam, and you will be just fine!

## A COMPARISON OF FAR, AUD, AND REG RESEARCH

Personally, I believe FAR is the most challenging of the research areas. FAR remains challenging because the standards are fairly complex. On the CPA exam, you should encounter one research question on each simulation. The research question requires you to transfer only one paragraph, so there will be *one* correct answer. If you attempt to paste a second paragraph, your first paragraph will automatically be deleted.

REG can be challenging if you have only taken one tax class and have not received any exposure to tax research. However, if you study Chapter 7, you should have a nice overview of the organization of the Code. Knowing the organization and structure of the Code should help you find your answer. Like the FAR exam, there should be one research question on each REG simulation. Similar to FAR, there is only *one* correct answer to each research question in REG. Again, if you attempt to paste a second paragraph into your answer, your first paragraph will automatically be deleted.

AUD can be more challenging because research can be tested in either a reporting requirement, a research question, or both. In addition, the research question may require you to paste one or more paragraphs for the answer. Make *sure* you read the instructions carefully in the audit simulation so you understand whether the answer requires one paragraph or more than one paragraph.

## LAST-MINUTE PREPARATIONS

Although you have spent time on the CPA sample exam, it's a good idea to visit the AICPA Web site about a week before the exam to be sure there are no new announcements or changes. You should look at the CPA exam Web site for any updates, breaking news, or alerts.

You should also revisit the sample exam approximately seven to ten days before the exam. You want to make sure the exam interface has not been changed or modified for your particular testing window. Read carefully all instructions on this sample exam. You also should practice using the interface just prior to taking the exam. Use the calculator again and try out all of its functions. You want to be fast and secure with the calculator so you can trust your skills and answers during the exam.

Also, do not forget to visit the AICPA Web site and read any alerts. If previous candidates had difficulty with any functions on the exam, sometimes the AICPA issues a clarification on their Web page.

### AT THE EXAM

Quickly read the instructions to make sure you are familiar with them and that none of them have changed. Pace yourself on each section. Watch your time. Know when it's time to move on! And most important of all, have *confidence* in yourself. Knowledge, confidence, and time management are key to success on the CPA exam. Have faith in your knowledge and skills and do your very best!

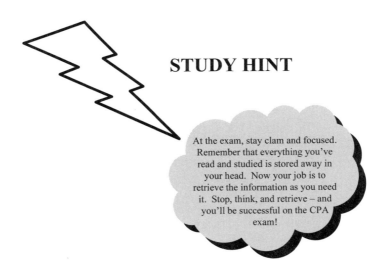

## STUDY HINT

At the exam, stay clam and focused. Remember that everything you've read and studied is stored away in your head. Now your job is to retrieve the information as you need it. Stop, think, and retrieve – and you'll be successful on the CPA exam!

# APPENDIX A

# IMPORTANT RESOURCES FOR THE CPA EXAM

The AICPA provides some important resources to help you prepare for the CPA exam. These resources are found at the AICPA Web site at www.cpa-exam.org.

It is important to understand what content is tested on the exam, how to apply for the exam, how to schedule your exam, and what to bring to the exam. In addition, it is important to understand the exam interface so that you do not lose valuable time on the exam learning navigation or commands.

Some candidates study with review materials that are not up-to-date, which can cause problems on the exam. It is important that you are current with the accounting literature. I always recommend that you buy the most recent version of the CPA review materials so that you are well prepared for the exam. However, if it has been six months since you have studied, or you are repeating a section of the exam, you may need to update yourself. If new standards have been issued, you will need to check the FASB Web site to download and learn the new standards. I have listed the Web sites for the FASB and the PCAOB so you can download the most recent literature.

Below is a list of the most important resources to help you prepare for the exam.

## CPA Candidate Bulletin

The *CPA Candidate Bulletin* is approximately 33 pages in length. It outlines the contents of the exam, the application process, the scheduling process, and the exam process. It provides a lengthy list of what you need to take to the exam, such as personal identification. This pamphlet is very clear on what is primary identification, what is secondary identification, and what are unacceptable forms of identification. It also has an extensive list on what items are prohibited in the exam.

The *CPA Candidate Bulletin* also has important information about receiving your scores. In addition, it discusses retaking the exam, and the examination content for each part.

The *CPA Candidate Bulletin* is a *must read* for all individuals taking the exam. It is very clear and well written. You should consult this bulletin prior to studying for the exam, and again prior to taking the exam.

## Content Specifications Outlines

The Content Specifications Outlines (CSOs) are also available at the AICPA Web site at www.cpa-exam.org. This document is a detailed listing of the specific content areas covered on each area of the CPA exam. I recommend looking at this list before studying, so that you have an overview to each test.  The CSO documents will help you focus your studies.

## CPA Exam Tutorial

The CPA Exam Tutorial is also available at the AICPA Web site at www.cpa-exam.org.  The tutorial outlines the various functions on the exam.  The tutorial will walk you through the various commands, menus, calculator functions, spreadsheet functions, and simulation design.  Although this is excellent for learning about the exam interface, you should also practice on the sample exam.

## CPA Sample Exam

The CPA Sample Exam is another valuable resource that will help you prepare for the exam.  This sample exam is invaluable in learning all the commands of the exam interface.  You can use the multiple-choice portion only, the simulation portion only, or the entire sample exam.

I recommend working with the multiple-choice portion first.  Learn how to mark questions for review, unmark them, work the calculator, etc.  Take some time with this and enter nonsensical data to see how the program responds.

I recommend working with the simulation portion separately.  You should use the calculator and spreadsheet and make up your own problems to gain experience with these tools.  You should also use the infobase extensively to practice the different kinds of searches.  Don't limit yourself to the research question on the sample exam.  Make up your own queries for another topic that is in that area of the infobase, and analyze the results.  Use the drop-down menus, the advanced search, and the simple search.  Analyze the difference in your results.  Use the infobase enough on the sample exam to give yourself confidence on the exam.

One important aspect of these sample exams is that the multiple-choice may be similar on all sections of the exam (FAR, AUD, REG, and BEC).  However, the simulations interface and research infobases will be different.  I strongly recommend that you work with each of these separately before you take each particular portion of the exam.

## FASB Web Site

The FASB Web site at www.fasb.org can be used to find any new pronouncements issued since your study materials were published.  First, check the date on the pronouncement.  Then, check the effective date and transition requirements.  If early application is permitted, the standard is testable six months after it is issued.

Some standards are technical and difficult to learn.  It is always a good idea to read the summary and the introduction, as well as any other front-end material in the newer standards. This introductory material is excellent for understanding the new standard. The introductory material also explains the changes that were made. After you have the "big picture" of the new standard, you can then skim the standard to see the organization of the new pronouncement and the most important rules.

**PCAOB Web Site**

The PCAOB Web site at www.pcaob.org is useful in finding any new auditing standards that are applicable to publicly traded companies. At the top of the page, there is a tab or button marked *Standards*. This Web site also has the interim standards posted, which are the AICPA professional standards. You can also use this Web site to practice auditing research (instead of using the AICPA Web site). The PCAOB Web site doesn't have the same search capabilities as the infobase search engines. However, the table of contents is available. Therefore, you can use this Web site to learn your way around the auditing and attestation standards.

# APPENDIX B

# HELPFUL HINTS FOR INFOBASES

## FARS CD-ROM, FARS ONLINE, AND AICPA ONLINE RESOURCE

### FARS CD-ROM

As we discussed in earlier chapters, the FARS CD-ROM product uses a Folio interface. The CD-ROM product with Folio Views is an excellent piece of software. You will enjoy using this program more if you understand how to use a few special features. Specifically, you need to understand the various panes or views, the jump links, the advanced search command, and Boolean operators.

Superseded material is shaded in gray. Amended material has a large black line to the left. When you see superseded or amended material, you should also see one or more red diamonds. A red diamond is a jump link that will take you to the updated portion of the infobase. These jump links are very well done and quite helpful.

You will also enjoy the program more if you know how to change a few of the default settings. I recommend changing two important settings: the contents setting and the hidden text setting.

### Views

Near the bottom of the screen, you will see five tabs: *Contents/Documents*, *Document*, *Contents*, *Hit List*, and *Object*. The first three are very helpful. Below is a list that outlines each view.

| Tab | Function |
|---|---|
| Contents/Document | Splits the screen and places contents on the left and the document on the right |
| Document | Displays the document |
| Contents | Displays expandable table of contents with your search results |

### Contents

In order to display the expandable contents showing the results of your search, you need to change one of the default settings. Follow this path through the menus and check the box that is titled "Query Results."

| | |
|---|---|
| Tools | |
|     Options | |
|         Contents | |
|             Query Results | |

## Hidden Text

Now let's change the setting so we can see the hidden text. This is important because it highlights the citation of each record immediately before the record. The citation is printed in blue. This is important because if you are cutting and pasting the record, it will allow the citation to be cut and pasted with the paragraph.

Follow this path through the menus and check the box that says "Hidden Text."

```
Tools
     Options
          Documents
               Hidden Text
```

## View All Records/View Records with Hits

Another important feature to understand in Folio is how to shift between *View All Records* and *View Records with Hits*. This is very powerful. By changing your view, you jump around in the infobase and read either the results or the area around your results. This comes in handy when your results or hits are close to what you are looking for, but not quite the right answer. You can move from viewing the search results into viewing the area in that particular standard by going to the top command line and changing your view from *View Records with Hits* to *View All Records*. The infobase will jump you to the full standard in which your cursor is positioned. Make sure you click into your paragraph so that your cursor is positioned in the correct place before you change to *View All Records*, or you'll land in the wrong standard. This is a powerful and fast way to get to the standard without going back through the table of contents! It makes research a *lot* faster! And it's fun!

## Arrow Keys

The three different sets of arrow keys are another fabulous feature in the FARS CD-ROM version of the infobase. You have three sets of arrows. The arrows on the far left side of the command bar are the *Go Back, Go Forward* commands. This takes you back one step or forward one step and will toggle you between different search results. If you go back too far, you'll hit the table of contents where you entered the infobase. Of course, you can move between the search results by using the menu at the top marked *Search* and *Show History*, but this is more time-consuming. The other two sets of arrow keys jump you from hit to hit (within the paragraph), or from record to record (paragraph to paragraph).

## Searches

There are two search commands: simple search and advanced search. The large binoculars begin an advanced search. The small binoculars begin a simple search. Stay away from simple search. The simple search only produces 50 results and these results are selected by some algorithm and prioritized. The results generated in a simple search are *not* a complete list of results. Therefore, simple searches are of limited value.

Use advanced search with the big binoculars on the toolbar. Advanced search gives you a word window on the left, and displays the number of hits found as you type in your query. Advanced search allows you to monitor the quantity of results as you type in your query. Advanced search also provides the researcher with a comprehensive search and complete results. In addition, the advanced search command allows you to use the Boolean operators to expand or narrow your search. Advanced search is the most powerful feature on the FARS-CD.

## Boolean Operators

Below is a list of the Boolean operators that can be used with the Folio interface. If you don't like memorizing the operator symbols, you can use language commands. You can find the instructions for doing this in FARS Help. Personally, I use the symbols because it's faster. There is also a drop-down menu with the operators, but that's also too time-consuming for my taste.

| Boolean Operators | Function |
|---|---|
| & | And |
| \| | Or |
| ^ | Not |
| ~ | Exclusive Or |
| * | Wildcard |
| / | Ordered Proximity |
| @ | Unordered Proximity |
| "xxx" | Character String Search |

The keywords in proximity searches should be in quotation marks with the / or @ symbol after it, and the number of words behind it. For example, if you search for "depreciation asset"/10, this will look for all paragraphs where the words *depreciation* and *asset* are found within 10 words of each other in that order. If you search for "depreciation asset"@10, this will find where the words *depreciation* and *asset* are within 10 words of each other in either order.

**Search Within**

The *Search Within* command is slightly more cumbersome to use in the FARS CD than it is in FARS Online. On the FARS CD, you need to be in the advanced search and use brackets to identify the area that you wish to search. I have only used the *Search Within* feature once or twice with the FARS CD. I find it more helpful to use an advanced search, bring up the results, then move to the contents window to look at the standard titles with the number of results, and then click on the standard. I think this strategy is much more powerful, because you do not narrow your search too early in the research process. You can see all the results everywhere in the infobase, and the results are clearly labeled. Then, you can choose the standard and look within that standard. If you click on the standard that shows the results, it takes you to the beginning of the standard. Then, you can use the arrow key to jump to the next hit and quickly find your search term within the standard.

Therefore, rather than searching within, you can look within *after* your search. To do this, perform a search and retrieve the results. Then, go to the contents pane and look at the numerical results found in each standard. Click on the standard that is most appropriate. It's fast and it's easy, and it saves time from doing multiple searches within because you can see the results all at once. Another fine feature of the FARS CD!

**FARS Online**

There is a beautiful online tutorial for the FARS Online site.

I recommend going to this site and quickly reading the contents of "How to Use FARS." It is usually found on the left-hand side of the screen when you enter the main page.

FARS Online is relatively easy to use, and it's very intuitive. Again, as we discussed in an earlier chapter, remember that the advanced keyword search jumbles up the results. If you want results in the same order as the infobase, use a simple search. To change the type of search, click on the *Search* tab and then go to the bottom of the page and you can change the search from simple to advanced or vice-versa.

An important point to make when comparing this infobase with the CPA sample exam is that the FARS Online infobase presents the results list with the name and number of the standard in which the hit was found. However, the results list in FARS Online is difficult to read because it uses full titles instead of abbreviations of the standards. Personally, I think these full citation titles clutter the screen and make it difficult to read the results. You will have to work with this infobase to become comfortable and gain speed in reading the results list.

Another important point to make is that although the search engines work similarly in FARS Online and the CPA sample exam, the display of the results list is considerably different. On the CPA sample exam, the results list displays the bold heading in the standard, and it does not indicate the standard number. You must click on the document in the results list and read the top of the document to determine the standard number. Clicking on each result and reading the beginning to identify the standard is incredibly time-consuming.

The document excerpt view (off, short, medium, and long) is on the right-hand corner of the results window in FARS Online. This feature is also similar to the CPA sample exam. In addition, both FARS Online and the CPA sample exam are programmed to search for documents. A document is normally several paragraphs under a bolded heading in the standards.

The search commands in FARS Online are also similar to the CPA exam interface. *Search Within* works in the same way on both of these infobases.

Similar to the FARS CD-ROM, the FARS Online infobase also has the appropriate jump links for superseded and amended material.

**AICPA onLine Resource**

At first, AICPA onLine Resource is a little tricky to find your way around and get the table of contents (TOC) opened. If the TOC is available when you open the program, use that. However, when you use the *Search* function, the TOC menu on the left disappears. If you use *Quick Find*, the TOC menu will reappear. Use *Quick Find* at the top of the screen, and then dig down into the TOC on the left, you'll begin to find your way around.

In order to read the full titles, you need to expand the table of contents titles. Unlike the CPA sample exam, you cannot click and drag the window open in the AICPA onLine infobase. You must use the button found at the top of the TOC, which is the black branching button to the far left of the ? sign. Click on the branching or outline symbol and wait for the left window to slowly expand. Again, on the CPA exam, you just click on the TOC and drag it open wider.

As you know, each infobase has slight differences in the commands. If you are trying to click on the TOC to get the AU menus to drop down, click on the + sign, not the document sign. If you click on the document, it just retrieves a document page and doesn't expand your TOC where you can read the titles. Keep clicking on the + sign and you can read the titles and sections to the various standards. When you reach the lowest document level for that particular standard (i.e., AT 301), you will see the descriptive titles for the bold headings in the standard. You can browse here until you find the right topic! This should be similar to what you will see in your TOC on the CPA exam.

Go ahead and compare this with the CPA sample exam TOC. You will see the similarities. The good news is that if you practice with the AICPA Web site when you receive your NTS, you will be able to see all the account titles and subtitles, and you will become very familiar with the AUs, the ARs, and the ATs.

The *Search* command on the AICPA onLine Resource produces results that are similar to the FARS Online and CPA sample exam search results: all jumbled up and listed by document. Again, the search results on the CPA sample exam appear slightly different, but they are essentially the same style results.

# APPENDIX C

# THE CPA SAMPLE EXAM INTERFACE

As we discussed in Chapter 8 and Appendix B, every piece of software will have its unique features. Some of these features are intuitive, and some are not. It is your responsibility to find out how everything works *before* you get into the exam. In this Appendix, I have listed some features of the CPA sample exam, and explained the challenges I have encountered when working with this sample exam. Enjoy!

## Entering Numbers or Values

Some answers require that you type in an amount. This makes the exam more like working a problem. The strange part is that when you are supposed to enter numbers, you click on the box in which you want to enter your answer. You think, I will type my answer, and it will appear in that box. No, no, no! That's not how it works.

When you click on the answer box, the outline of the box turns white. When you start typing in numbers, it jumps up to an input line at the top of the answer area. Your answer doesn't appear in the answer box until you hit enter. Then the answer jumps from the white input area at the top and lands in the orange box. Be careful here, because it is easy to make a typographical error at the top, hit enter, and not realize you put in the wrong number. Proof the number after it is entered.

## Cut, Copy, Paste, and Delete

Interestingly enough, in some parts of the sample exam, you can right click, and you will find some commands. While entering numbers, a right click on the mouse may access a drop-down menu to copy, paste, and delete. This little menu also says that you can copy by pressing CTRL+C and paste by pressing Ctrl+V. You can clear the input area by using the Del key. Oddly enough, I did not get these same commands with my right click when I was in the Communications or other parts of the exam. So, be careful— the commands do not always work uniformly in the various parts of the exam.

Another unusual function I found was when I was at the top of the screen in the data entry line for entering numbers, a right click opens a drop-down menu with a list of functions such as Undo, Cut, Copy, Paste, Delete, and Select All. I am not sure if these are necessary or useful on the exam, but they were on the sample exam. Therefore, these same functions should also be available on the CPA exam.

A third place for the Cut, Copy, and Paste commands in the simulations is in the upper right-hand corner of the chart or table that requires completion. You see a Copy, Cut, and Paste command at the top of the answer area for the particular problem. Normally, you see this feature in areas that require journal entries or problems that require insertion of numbers into tables.

**Fill in the Blanks**

Other parts of the simulations require you to use a drop-down menu to select answers from a given list. This essentially turns the question into a multiple-choice question. On these fill-in questions, if you click once, the box turns yellow. Click again, and the answers pop up on your screen. You select your answer by highlighting it, and then click "OK." Your answer will be inserted into the box.

**Journal Entries**

Entering journal entries also has some interesting features. First, there is only one column for the account titles. The account titles are usually chosen from a drop-down menu. However, the account titles for the credit entry cannot be indented. For the amounts, there are Debit and Credit columns that are properly indented. Be sure to place your debit or credit in the appropriate column.

The lack of a debit/credit distinction in the account titles makes your answer more difficult to analyze and proofread, because as accountants we *always* indent both the title and the amount for the credit entry. From a practical perspective, it is difficult to work with an interface on the exam that is not formatted correctly, but that is the way the exam was programmed. Be extra careful that you place the credit amount in the correct column!

Another point to make about the journal entries is that there is nothing built into the system to force you to balance. As an accountant you should be intelligent enough to check your journal entries and make *sure* every entry balances. If you have been working in industry with accounting software that displays an error message for entries that don't balance, don't expect this to happen on the CPA exam. Check your answer and make *sure* each entry balances!

**The Calculator**

The calculator is at the top right-hand corner of your screen, and you can drop it down and move it around within your testing area. Just click on it and drag it where you want it. As you know, it's a simple calculator with the functions of add, subtract, multiply, divide, and square root.

Unlike some calculators, the numbers you need to add (or multiply) together will not show on the input line of the calculator. Only one input number shows, not the entire equation. So if you want to add 1 + 2 = 3, the calculator will not display the items added or the equation. You type in 1, then you press +, then type in 2, then hit equal, and the answer 3 shows up. Very simple, but sometimes you feel as if you are working blind. Practice with the calculator until you develop speed and proficiency. You should enter the exam room feeling comfortable with the calculator like it is an old friend!

The calculator on the sample exam contains a fascinating feature. Even though the calculator does not have an $x^y$ key, you can manually perform this operation by entering in your first equation, and then hitting the equal sign (=) repeatedly. Try this: 3 x 3 will equal 9. Then hit = again, and you get 27. Then hit = again, you'll get 81. So basically each time you hit the equal sign for a number times itself, you are raising it to another power. Try this!

This feature also works with the divide sign, where you can generate present value factors by yourself without a table. Key in the following: 1 ÷ 1.10 will equal .909090 (repeating). This is the present value factor at 10% for one period. Then hit = again. It divides your last result by 1.10, which gives you $1 \div 1.10^2$ which is .82644. This number is the PV factor at 10% for two periods. If you hit = again, it brings it back 3 periods.

Why is this feature important? Sometimes in the multiple-choice problems, they give you only a part of the PV table, or part of a PVA table. Sometimes they give you a PVA due table instead of a regular PVA table. Knowing how to do this quickly on the calculator will allow you to check your work. You can quickly generate your own PV or PVA table. To make a PVA table, you must add the PV factors. Try this on the sample exam with a PV table handy so you can check your work! It's a nice little trick!

I would also recommend that you extensively use the calculator on the sample exam and try all the memory functions. When I have my favorite calculator with me in class, I feel more comfortable working problems. When I forget my calculator and borrow someone's calculator, I don't feel as secure with a strange calculator. Quite honestly, when I borrow a calculator and I am not comfortable with the keyboard, I make more mistakes. The same thing will happen to you on the CPA exam. Therefore, make sure you use the computer calculator extensively. Be sure to find your comfort level with the on-screen calculator before you sit for the CPA exam. Speed and agility are important here. Become pals with your online calculator!

Some CPA candidates have told me that they didn't practice very much with the calculator because there were only five multiple-choice sample questions. Do not limit yourself only to the practice problems provided with the same exam. Use that calculator for whatever you want! I opened the sample exam and used the calculator several times for regular homework in the classes I teach. Sometimes I would open the sample exam and make up numbers and play with the calculator for about an hour or so until I knew what it would do.

So, use the calculator extensively on the sample exam, and you'll feel like an expert when the time comes to use that online calculator!

## Spreadsheet Functions

The spreadsheet functions may not work exactly like the spreadsheet functions in Excel. You should check your Resources tab for the spreadsheet formulas in the sample exam, and then practice with various formulas before you take the exam.

## Communications

Beware that the input entry for your memo will expand (perhaps infinitely) to accommodate either your creative brilliance or your lack thereof. Avoid the urge to become verbose just because the space expands to fit your needs. Your best strategy is to outline quickly the key points you want to make, and then write your memo. Remember, it's a professional memo. No slang!

Avoid the temptation to open the infobase and copy or paste something from the infobase. The AICPA has commented on their Web site that some candidates have been copying and pasting research answers into the communications component. The communications components exist to grade *your* writing; therefore, the answer should be in your own words.

Also, proof your memo for key items such as subject-verb agreement, dangling modifiers, spelling, etc. I've heard reports from candidates that sometimes the spell-checker works, sometimes it doesn't. If the spell-checker doesn't work, make sure you report it to the test center and the AICPA immediately after the exam. Instructions for reporting problems with the test and software are found at the AICPA Web site in the *CPA Candidate Bulletin*.

## Research

We talked about these special commands and differences in infobases in Chapters 8 and 9. Make sure you understand this information, and make sure you practice with the CPA sample exam *before* you take each part of the exam. This interface is significantly different from the commercially available software, so it helps to practice with the sample exam. Be *sure* to follow the special instructions and split the screen so you can highlight and transfer your answer.

# APPENDIX D

# QUICK STUDY LISTS FOR FAR, AUD, AND REG

## FINANCIAL ACCOUNTING AND REPORTING

| Accounting Research Bulletin Quick Study List | | |
|---|---|---|
| *Number* | *Topic* | *Explanation of Contents* |
| ARB 43 | Restatement and Revision of ARBs | Prior Opinions, Forms of Statements, working capital, inventory pricing, capital accounts, depreciation, property taxes, government contracts |
| ARB 45 | Long-Term Construction-Type Contracts | Percentage of completion method and completed contract |
| ARB 46 | Discontinuance of Dating Earned Surplus | Amendment to quasi-reorganization material in ARB 43 |
| ARB 51 | Consolidated Financial Statements | Intercompany transactions, minority interests (until effect date of FAS 160), and combined statements in effect. FAS 141 supersedes remaining items. |

| APB Opinions Quick Study List | |
|---|---|
| *Number* | *Topic* |
| APB 6 | Status of Accounting Research Bulletins |
| APB 9 | Reporting the Results of Operations |
| APB 10 | Omnibus Opinion—1966 |
| APB 12 | Omnibus Opinion—1967 |
| APB 14 | Accounting for Convertible Debt and Debt Issued with Stock Purchase Warrants |
| APB 18 | The Equity Method of Accounting for Investments in Common Stock |
| APB 21 | Interest on Receivables and Payables |
| APB 22 | Disclosure of Accounting Policies |
| APB 26 | Early Extinguishment of Debt |
| APB 28 | Interim Financial Reporting |
| APB 29 | Accounting for Nonmonetary Transactions |
| APB 30 | Reporting the Results of Operations—Discontinued Events and Extraordinary Items |

| FASB Statements Quick Study List | |
|---|---|
| *Number* | *Title of Standards* |
| FAS 2 | Accounting for Research and Development Costs |
| FAS 5 | Accounting for Contingencies |
| FAS 6 | Classification of Short-Term Obligations Expected to Be Refinanced |
| FAS 13 | Accounting for Leases |
| FAS 15 | Accounting by Debtors and Creditors for Troubled Debt Restructurings |
| FAS 16 | Prior Period Adjustments |
| FAS 23 | Inception of the Lease |
| FAS 27 | Classification of Renewals or Extensions of Existing Sales-Type or Direct Financing Leases |
| FAS 28 | Accounting for Sales with Leasebacks |
| FAS 29 | Determining Contingent Rentals |
| FAS 34 | Capitalization of Interest Cost |
| FAS 43 | Accounting for Compensated Absences |
| FAS 45 | Accounting for Franchise Fee Revenue |
| FAS 47 | Disclosure of Long-Term Obligations |
| FAS 48 | Revenue Recognition When Right of Return Exists |
| FAS 49 | Accounting for Product Financing Arrangements |
| FAS 52 | Foreign Currency Translation |
| FAS 57 | Related-Party Disclosures |
| FAS 58 | Capitalization of Interest Cost in Financial Statements That Include Investments Accounted for by the Equity Method |
| FAS 66 | Accounting for Sales of Real Estate |
| FAS 67 | Accounting for Costs and Initial Rental Operations of Real Estate Projects |
| FAS 68 | Research and Development Arrangements |
| FAS 78 | Classification of Obligations That Are Callable by the Creditor |
| FAS 84 | Induced Conversions of Convertible Debt |
| FAS 86 | Accounting for the Costs of Computer Software to Be Sold, Leased, or Otherwise Marketed |
| FAS 87 | Employers' Accounting for Pensions |
| FAS 88 | Employers' Accounting for Settlements & Curtailments of Defined Benefit Pension Plans and for Termination Benefits |
| FAS 89 | Financial Reporting and Changing Prices |
| FAS 91 | Nonrefundable Fees & Costs Associated with Originating or Acquiring Loans and Initial Direct Costs of Leases |
| FAS 94 | Consolidation of All Majority-Owned Subsidiaries |
| FAS 95 | Statement of Cash Flows |
| FAS 98 | Accounting for Leases |
| FAS 106 | Employers' Accounting for Postretirement Benefits other than Pensions |

| Number | Title of Standards |
|--------|-------------------|
| FAS 107 | Disclosures about Fair Value of Financial Instruments |
| FAS 109 | Accounting for Income Taxes |
| FAS 112 | Employers' Accounting for Postemployment Benefits |
| FAS 114 | Accounting by Creditors for Impairment of a Loan |
| FAS 115 | Accounting for Certain Investments in Debt and Equity Securities |
| FAS 116 | Accounting for Contributions Received and Contributions Made |
| FAS 118 | Accounting by Creditors for Impairment of a Loan— Income Recognition and Disclosures |
| FAS 123(R) | Share-Based Payment |
| FAS 128 | Earnings Per Share |
| FAS 129 | Disclosure of Information about Capital Structure |
| FAS 130 | Reporting Comprehensive Income |
| FAS 131 | Disclosures about Segments of an Enterprise and Related Information |
| FAS 132(R) | Employers' Disclosures about Pensions and Other Postretirement Benefits—an Amendment of FASB Statements No. 87, 88, and 106 |
| FAS 133 | Accounting for Derivative Instruments and Hedging Activities |
| FAS 138 | Accounting for Certain Derivative Instruments and Certain Hedging Activities—an Amendment of FASB Statement No. 133 |
| FAS 139 | Rescission of FASB Statement No. 53 and Amendments to FASB Statements No. 63, 89, and 121 |
| FAS 140 | Accounting for Transfers and Servicing of Financial Assets and Extinguishments of Liabilities |
| FAS 141 | Business Combinations |
| FAS 142 | Goodwill and Other Intangible Assets |
| FAS 143 | Accounting for Asset Retirement Obligations |
| FAS 144 | Accounting for the Impairment or Disposal of Long-Lived Assets |
| FAS 145 | Rescission of FASB Statements 4, 44, and 64, Amendment of FASB Statement No. 13, and Technical Corrections |
| FAS 146 | Accounting for Costs Associated with Exit or Disposal Activities |
| FAS 149 | Amendment of FASB Statement No. 133 on Derivative and Hedging Activities |
| FAS 150 | Accounting for Certain Financial Instruments with Characteristics of Both Liabilities and Equity |
| FAS 151 | Inventory Costs—an Amendment of ARB 43, Chapter 4 |
| FAS 152 | Accounting for Real Estate Time-Sharing Transactions |
| FAS 153 | Exchanges of Nonmonetary Assets—an Amendment of APB Opinion 29 |
| FAS 154 | Accounting Changes and Error Correction |

| Number | Title of Standards |
| --- | --- |
| FAS 155 | Accounting for Certain Hybrid Financial Instruments |
| FAS 156 | Accounting for Servicing of Financial Assets |
| FAS 157 | Fair Value Measurements |
| FAS 158 | Employers' Accounting for Defined Benefit Pension and Other Postretirement Plans |
| FAS 159 | The Fair Value Option for Financial Assets and Financial Liabilities |
| FAS 160 | Noncontrolling Interests in Consolidated Financial Statements—an Amendment or ARB 51 Combinations (Effective for fiscal years beginning after December 15, 2008) |
| FAS 141(R) | Business Combinations (Effective for fiscal years beginning after December 15, 2008) |

AUDITING AND ATTESTATION

| PCAOB Standards Quick Study List As of January 2008 | |
|---|---|
| *Number* | *Title* |
| AS 1 | References in Auditors' Report to the Standards of the PCAOB |
| AS 2 | An Audit of Internal Control over Financial Reporting Performed in Conjunction with an Audit of Financial Statements |
| AS 3 | Audit Documentation |
| AS 4 | Reporting on Whether a Previously Reported Material Weakness Continues to Exist (effective February 6, 2006) |
| AS 5 | An Audit of Internal Control over Financial Reporting That Is Integrated with an Audit of Financial Statements (effective for fiscal years ending on or after November 15, 2007) |

| AICPA Professional Standards List of Prefixes | |
|---|---|
| *Prefix* | *Topic* |
| None | Applicability of AICPA Professional Standards and PCAOB Standards |
| AU | Statements on Auditing Standards and Related Auditing Interpretations |
| RULE | Select SEC-Approved PCAOB |
| AT | Statements on Standards for Attestation Engagements and Related Attest Engagement Interpretations |
| AR | Statements on Standards for Accounting and Review Services and Related Accounting and Review Services Interpretations |
| ET | Code of Professional Conduct |
| BL | Bylaws |
| CS | Consulting Services |
| QC | Quality Control |
| PR | Peer Review |
| TS | Tax Services |
| PFP | Personal Financial Planning |
| CPE | Continuing Professional Education |

## Auditing

| US Auditing Standards Quick Study List AUs | |
|---|---|
| *Number* | *Title* |
| AU 100 | Introduction |
| AU 200 | The General Standards |
| AU 300 | The Standards of Fieldwork |
| AU 400 | The First, Second, and Third Standards of Reporting |

| Number | Title |
|--------|-------|
| AU 500 | The Fourth Standard of Reporting |
| AU 600 | Other Types of Reports |
| AU 700 | Special Topics |
| AU 800 | Compliance Auditing |
| AU 900 | Special Reports of the Committee on Auditing Procedures |

| | Auditing Standards<br>Statements on Auditing Standards—Introduction<br>100 Series |
|--------|-------|
| Number | Title |
| 110 | Responsibilities and Functions of the Independent Auditor |
| 120 | Defining Professional Requirements in Statements on Auditing Standards |
| 150 | Generally Accepted Auditing Standards |
| 161 | The Relationship of Generally Accepted Auditing Standards to Quality Control Standards |

| | Auditing Standards<br>The General Standards<br>200 Series |
|--------|-------|
| Number | Title |
| 201 | Nature of the General Standards |
| 210 | Training and Proficiency of the Independent Auditor |
| 220 | Independence |
| 230 | Due Professional Care in the Performance of Work |

| | Auditing Standards<br>The Standards of Fieldwork<br>300 Series |
|--------|-------|
| Number | Title |
| 310 | Appointment of the Independent Auditor |
| 311 | Planning and Supervision |
| 312 | Audit Risk and Materiality |
| 313 | Substantive Tests Prior to the Balance Sheet Date |
| 314 | Understanding the Entity and Its Environment and Assessing the Risks of Material Misstatement |
| 315 | Communications between Predecessor and Successor Auditors |
| 316 | Consideration of Fraud in a Financial Statement Audit |
| 317 | Illegal Acts by Clients |
| 318 | Performing Audit Procedures in Response to Assessed Risks and Evaluating the Audit Evidence Obtained |
| 319 | Consideration of Internal Control in a Financial Statement Audit |
| 322 | Auditor's Consideration of the Internal Audit Function in an Audit of Financial Statements |
| 324 | Service Organizations |

| Number | Title |
|--------|-------|
| 325 | Communication of Internal Control Related Matters Noted in an Audit |
| 326 | Audit Evidence |
| 328 | Auditing Fair Value Measurements and Disclosures |
| 329 | Analytical Procedures |
| 330 | The Confirmation Process |
| 331 | Inventories |
| 332 | Auditing Derivative Instruments, Hedging Activities, and Investments in Securities |
| 333 | Management Representations |
| 334 | Related Parties |
| 336 | Using the Work of a Specialist |
| 337 | Inquiry of a Client's Lawyer Concerning Litigation, Claims, and Assessments |
| 339 | Audit Documentation |
| 341 | The Auditor's Consideration of an Entity's Ability to Continue as a Going Concern |
| 342 | Auditing Accounting Estimates |
| 350 | Audit Sampling |
| 380 | The Auditor's Communication with Those Charged with Governance |
| 390 | Consideration of Omitted Procedures after the Report Date |

| Auditing Standards The First, Second, and Third Standards of Reporting 400 Series | |
|--------|-------|
| Number | Title |
| 410 | Adherence to GAAP |
| 411 | The Meaning of Present Fairly in Conformity with GAAP |
| 420 | Consistency of Application of GAAP |
| 431 | Adequacy of Disclosure in Financial Statements |
| 435 | Segment Information (Rescinded by the Auditing Standards Board) |

| Auditing Standards The Fourth Standard of Reporting 500 Series | |
|--------|-------|
| Number | Title |
| 504 | Association with Financial Statements |
| 508 | Reports on Audited Financial Statements |
| 530 | Dating of the Independent Auditor's Report |
| 532 | Restricting the User of an Auditor's Report |
| 534 | Reporting on Financial Statements Prepared for Use in Other Countries |
| 543 | Part of Audit Performed by Other Independent Auditors |

| Number | Title |
|---|---|
| 544 | Lack of Conformity with Generally Accepted Accounting Principles |
| 550 | Other Information in Documents Containing Audited Financial Statements |
| 551 | Reporting on Information Accompanying the Basic Financial Statements in Auditor-Submitted Documents |
| 552 | Reporting on Condensed Financial Statements and Selected Financial Data |
| 558 | Required Supplementary Information |
| 560 | Subsequent Events |
| 561 | Subsequent Discovery of Facts Existing at the Date of the Auditor's Report |

## Attestation

| Attestation Engagements Study List | |
|---|---|
| Number | Title |
| AT 20 | Defining Professional Requirements in Statements on Standards for Attestation Engagements |
| AT 50 | SSAE Hierarchy |
| AT 101 | Attest Engagements |
| AT 201 | Agreed-Upon Procedures Engagements |
| AT 301 | Financial Forecasts and Projections |
| AT 401 | Reporting on Pro Forma Financial Information |
| AT 501 | Reporting on an Entity's Internal Control over Financial Reporting |
| AT 601 | Compliance Attestation |
| AT 701 | Management's Discussion and Analysis |

## Accounting and Review

| Accounting and Review Services Study List | |
|---|---|
| Number | Title |
| AR 50 | Standards for Accounting and Review Services |
| AR 100 | Compilation and Review of Financial Statements |
| AR 110 | Compilation of Specified Elements, Accounts, or Items of a Financial Statement |
| AR 120 | Compilation of Pro Forma Financial Information |
| AR 200 | Reporting on Comparative Financial Statements |
| AR 300 | Compilation Reports on Financial Statements Included in Certain Prescribed Forms |
| AR 400 | Communications between Predecessor and Successor Accountants |
| AR 600 | Reporting on Personal Financial Statements Included in Written Personal Financial Plans |

**REGULATION**

| | Internal Revenue Code<br>Subtitle A—Income Taxes<br>Quick Study List | |
|---|---|---|
| *Subchapter* | *Topic* | *Section Numbers* |
| A | Determination of Tax Liability | §1-59 |
| B | Computation of Taxable Income | §61-291 |
| C | Corporate Distributions and Adjustments | §300s |
| D | Deferred Compensation, etc. | §401-424 |
| E | Accounting Periods and Methods of Accounting | §441-483 |
| F | Exempt Organizations | §501-530 |
| G | Corporations Used to Avoid Income Tax on Shareholders | §531-565 |
| J | Estates, Trusts, Beneficiaries, and Decedents | §641-692 |
| K | Partners and Partnerships | §700s |
| N | Tax Based on Income from Sources within or without the United States | §861-999 |
| O | Gain or Loss on Disposition of Property | §1000s |
| P | Capital Gains and Losses | §1200s |
| Q | Readjustment of Tax between Years and Special Limitations | §1301-1351 |
| S | Tax Treatment of S Corporations and Their Shareholders | §1361-1379 |

| | Internal Revenue Code<br>Subtitles B and F<br>Quick Study List | |
|---|---|---|
| *Subtitle* | *Topic* | *Section Numbers* |
| **B** | Estate and Gift Taxes | |
| Chapter 11 | Estate Tax | §2000, §2100, §2200 series |
| Chapter 12 | Gift Tax | §2500 series |
| Chapter 13 | Tax on Generation-Skipping Transfers | §2600 series |
| Chapter 14 | Special Valuation Rules | §2700 series |
| **F** | Procedure and Administration | §6000 and §7000 series |

| Publication 17<br>Your Federal Income Tax | | |
|---|---|---|
| *Part* | *Number* | *Topic* |
| **One** | | **The Income Tax Return** |
| | 1 | Filing Information |
| | 2 | Filing Status |
| | 3 | Personal Exemptions and Dependents |
| | 4 | Tax Withholding and Estimated Tax |
| **Two** | | **Income** |
| | 5 | Wages, Salaries, and Other Earnings |
| | 6 | Tip Income |
| | 7 | Interest Income |
| | 8 | Dividends and Other Corporate Distributions |
| | 9 | Rental Income and Expenses |
| | 10 | Retirement Plans, Pensions, and Annuities |
| | 11 | Social Security and Equivalent Railroad Retirement Benefits |
| | 12 | Other Income |
| **Three** | | **Gains and Losses** |
| | 13 | Basis of Property |
| | 14 | Sale of Property |
| | 15 | Selling Your Home |
| | 16 | Reporting Gains and Losses |
| **Four** | | **Adjustments to Income** |
| | 17 | Individual Retirement Arrangements |
| | 18 | Alimony |
| | 19 | Education-Related Adjustments |
| **Five** | | **Standard Deduction and Itemized Deductions** |
| | 20 | Standard Deduction |
| | 21 | Medical and Dental Expenses |
| | 22 | Taxes |
| | 23 | Interest Expense |
| | 24 | Contributions |
| | 25 | Nonbusiness Casualty and Theft Losses |
| | 26 | Car Expenses and Other Employee Business Expense |
| | 27 | Tax Benefits for Work-Related Education |
| | 28 | Miscellaneous Deductions |
| | 29 | Limit on Itemized Deductions |
| **Six** | | **Figuring Your Taxes and Credits** |
| | 30 | How to Figure Your Tax |
| | 31 | Tax on Investment Income of Certain Minor Children |
| | 32 | Child and Dependent Care Credit |
| | 33 | Credit for the Elderly or the Disabled |
| | 34 | Child Tax Credit |
| | 35 | Education Credits |
| | 36 | Earned Income Credit |
| | 37 | Other Credits |

# APPENDIX E

# SOLUTIONS TO CHAPTER TESTS

## CHAPTER 1 TEST YOURSELF

**1.** (c) Research is tested on FAR, AUD and REG.

**2.** (b) The AICPA Professional Standards are tested in the AUD portion of the CPA exam.

**3.** (a) In FAR, the financial accounting standards are tested. The financial accounting standards are found in the FARS (Financial Accounting Research System) infobase.

**4.** (c) A simulation on AUD may contain a research component AND a report-writing component. The report-writing component may require a candidate to select up to ten paragraphs from the infobase to write a letter or report.

**5.** (d) Publication 17 is a document of the Department of the Treasury Internal Revenue Service (IRS).

**6.** (e) The FASB standards are available in hard paper copy, on CD, online, and at the FASB Web site. Only the FARS CD and FARS Online are in keyword searchable form.

**7.** (b) False. The FASB statements located at the FASB Web site are the pronouncements as they were originally issued. The FASB Statements are downloaded in Adobe .pdf format, but are not in a keyword searchable form.

**8.** (b) False. The FASB standards at the Web site are not updated for changes. The FASB standards at the FASB Web site are the pronouncements as they were originally issued.

**9.** (a) True. Publication 17 is entitled "Your Federal Income Tax for Individuals" and contains important information regarding amounts for deductions, exclusions, and limits on certain deductions.

**10.** (b) False. The AICPA only provides the CPA candidate with a version of FARS and a version of the AICPA Professional Standards. The financial accounting literature is used on the FAR portion of the exam; the AICPA Professional Standards are used on the AUD portion of the exam. A candidate can obtain access to this literature for six months after receiving their notice to schedule.

## CHAPTER 2 TEST YOURSELF

**1.** **(b)** False. The Original Pronouncements as Amended should not contain any outdated material. All amendments should be made, and all superseded material should be omitted. However, the version on the CPA exam may not omit all superseded material. In the sample exam, some superseded material has been included, so watch out for superseded material on the exam. Never cite superseded material.

**2.** **(b)** False. Searching both infobases will produce more results to read and can be very time-consuming for the candidate. The candidate should become proficient with either the Original Pronouncements or the Current Text and search with the infobase most familiar.

**3.** **(b)** False. The FASB Web site contains the most recent pronouncements. Pronouncements are not updated.

**4.** **(b)** False. The FASB Concept Statements (SFACs) are the lowest level priority in GAAP.

**5.** **(b)** The Accounting Reasearch Bulletins (ARBs) are included in Category A, which is the highest level priority in GAAP. The SFACs are Category E, the lowest priority. The AICPA Interpretations are Category D, the second lowest level of priority, and the AICPA SOPs are Category B, the second highest level of priority.

**6.** **(d)** The oldest GAAP is located in the Accounting Research Bulletins or ARBs.

**7.** **(b)** The Accounting Principles Board Opinions or the APBs contain opinion paragraphs that contain the accounting rules.

**8.** **(c)** The scope of a pronouncement explains the kinds of transactions covered by the accounting standard.

**9.** **(c)** Footnote disclosures are usually found at the end of an accounting standard, before the effective date and transition requirements, and before the appendices.

**10.** **(a)** F10.108 is a citation from the Current Text. This particular citation is on fair value option for financial assets and financial liabilities. ARB 43, par. 7, is from the Original Pronouncements. FIN 35, par. 3, is a citation from a FASB Interpretation. FAS 5, par. 12, is a citation from a FASB Statement.

## CHAPTER 3 TEST YOURSELF

**1.** **(b)** There are four ARBs that have not yet been superseded. These are ARB 43, 45, 46, and 51.

**2.** **(d)** Accounting rules are found in the "opinion" section of the APB Opinions. This is easy to remember because the standards of the Accounting Principles Board are called APB Opinions. The discussion often explains how to apply the rule. The introduction explains the overall accounting standard. The definitions outline any specialized vocabulary terms used in the standard.

**3.** **(a)** The two Ominibus Opinions are APB 10 and APB 12. APB 10 is mostly superseded and contains an amendment to ARB 43 on installment accounting. APB 12 is the Omnibus Act that contains many detailed rules on presentation of allowance accounts on the financial statements, accounting for deferred compensation for employees and surviving spouses, depreciation disclosures in the notes to financial statements, and the required disclosures for owners' equity.

**4.** **(c)** APB 30 contains the accounting rules for extraordinary items. APB 22 is the standard on accounting policy disclosures. APB 29 is the standard on non-monetary exchanges. APB 6 is the standard on the status of ARBs and contains the rules for Treasury stock, as well as presentation of current assets, current liabilities, and unearned discounts on the financial statements.

**5.** **(d)** APB 22 is the standard that outlines the rules for disclosing accounting policies in the notes to the financial statements. Answer (a) is incorrect because APB 6 outlines various rules for Treasury stock and stockholders' equity. Answer (b) is incorrect because ARB 43 is the restatement and revision of previous ARBs. Answer (c) is incorrect because ARB 51 is the standard that outlines rules for intercompany transactions of consolidated entities.

**6.** **(b)** ARB 43, Chapter 3 contains the definitions of working capital, current as-

sets, and current liabilities. APB 18 covers the equity method of accounting. ARB 51 covers intercompany transactions for consolidated entities, and APB 21 covers accounts receivable and accounts payable.

**7.** **(d)** APB 26 outlines the rules for early extinguishment of debt for the **debtor**. Note that FAS 114 includes the rules for the credit.

**8.** **(d)** The accounting rules for discontinued operations are now in the back of FAS 144. Although the title of APB 30 indicates that the rules for discontinued events are covered in APB 30, this part of the standard has been superseded.

**9.** **(d)** FAS 159 is the standard that outlines the fair value option for recording financial assets and financial liabilities. Because Beach elects the fair value option, the rules of FAS 159 will apply instead of the equity method rules contained in APB 18.

**10.** **(c)** The rules for Treasury stock transactions and recording gains on Treasury stock are found in APB 6.

## CHAPTER 3 PRACTICE YOUR RESEARCH SKILLS

1. APB 30, par. 23

2. ARB 43, Ch. 3A, par. 4

3. APB 30, par. 20

4. APB 12, par. 5

5. ARB 43, Ch. 7B, par. 2 (notice the term is stock split up)

6. ARB 43, Ch. 3A, par. 7

7. ARB 43, Ch. 7B, par. 10

8. APB 12, par. 3

9. ARB 43, Ch. 4, Statement 6

10. APB 29, par. 21

## CHAPTER 4  TEST YOURSELF

1. c

2. a

3. c

4. b

5. c

6. c

7. a

8. c

9. d

10. b

## CHAPTER 4  PRACTICE YOUR RESEARCH

1. FAS 13, par. 10

2. FAS 109, par. 41

3. FAS 157, par. 5

4. FAS 109, par. 42

5. FAS 115, par. 6

6. FAS 5, par. 17

7. FAS 13, par. 5d

8. FAS 45, par. 5

9. FAS 128, par. 13

10. FAS 154, par. 19

# CHAPTER 5  TEST YOURSELF

1. d

2. c

3. d

4. a

5. a

6. d

7. b

8. c

9. b

10. c

# CHAPTER 5 PRACTICE YOUR RESEARCH SKILLS

1. FAS 87, par. 20

2. FAS 52, par. 5

3. FAS 48, par. 6

4. 142, par. 18

5. FAS 13, par. 5(b), or FAS 23, par. 6 (which amended FAS 13, par. 5(b))

6. ARB 45, par. 4

7. ARB 43, Ch. 4, Statement 4

8. ARB 43, Ch. 4, Statement 9

9. APB 18, par. 19(c)

10. APB 21, par. 11

## CHAPTER 6  TEST YOURSELF

1. d
2. c
3. b
4. d
5. d
6. b
7. d
8. a
9. c
10. b

## CHAPTER 6  PRACTICE YOUR RESEARCH

1. AU 314.21
2. AU 319.63
3. AR 100.04
4. AU 508.58
5. AU 316.05
6. AU 319.07
7. AU 350.12
8. AT 301.09
9. AU 325.05
10. AU 329.04

# CHAPTER 7  TEST YOURSELF

1. c

2. a

3. d

4. c

5. b

6. d

7. c

8. a

9. a

10. d

# CHAPTER 7  PRACTICE YOUR RESEARCH SKILLS

1. §61(a). Yes, the dividend should be included as income.

2. §103(a). No, the interest on municipal bond is not included in the tax return.

3. §703(a). No, the partnership cannot deduct a charitable contribution. It must be reported on the K-1 for each partner and filed on the individual partner's Form 1040.

4. §166(a). $800 is the amount of deduction for tax purposes, which is the actual accounts that were not collected.

5. §162(f). No, fines may not be deducted for federal income tax purposes.

6. §172(b). Carry back 2 years, carry forward 20 years.

7. §705(a).

8. §1361(b). The maximum number of shareholders is 100.

9. §1211(b). Sheryl may deduct a capital loss of $8,000, which is the capital loss of $5,000 plus $3,000. (This tax rule is based on tax laws in effect as of January 2008.)

10. §11(b). The tax rate is 34% for Huffman. (This tax rate is based on tax laws in effect as of January 2008.)

authoritative literature for, 3–5. *See also* Financial Accounting Research System

as most challenging area, 144

quick study lists for, 161–164

research component for, 1, 2

research strategy for, 90

using sample exam for, 5

**Financial Accounting Research System (FARS), 15–29**

APBs, 26, 34–43

ARBs, 25–26, 31–34

CD and Online infobases, 16–17. *See also* FARS CD-ROM; FARS Online

comparing versions of, 4–5

Current Text, 18, 23–24. *See also* Current Text

difference between OPs and CT, 21–22

differences among versions of, 15

efficient use of OPs, 22–23

EITF Abstracts, 18

FASB Statements, 26–28. *See also* FASB Statements

hierarchy of GAAP, 20–21

Implementation Guides, 18

importance of standards' structure, 28–29

infobase of, 2

organization of OPs, 24–25

Original Pronouncements, 17–20

printed versions of literature, 15

topical coverage of. *See* Linkages among standards

**Financial Accounting Standards Board (FASB), 2**

pronouncements of, 17, 19

Web site of, 3, 11, 12, 15, 148–149

**Financial assets:**

*Accounting for Servicing of Financial Assets* (FAS 156), 64

*Accounting for Transfers and Servicing of Financial Assets and Extinguishment of Liabilities* (FAS 140), 88–89

*The Fair Value Option for Financial Assets and Financial Liabilities* (FAS 159), 66, 83–84

**Financial instruments, hybrid, 64**

**Financial liabilities, fair value option for, 66, 83–84**

**Financial reporting:**

*Interim Financial Reporting* (APB 28), 41

**Financial statements:**

*Balance Sheet Classification of Deferred Income Taxes* (FAS 37), 53

consolidated, 67, 84–85

*Noncontrolling Interests in Consolidated Financial Statements—an Amendment of ARB 51 Combinations* (FAS 160), 67

*The First, Second, and Third Standards of Reporting* **(AU 400), 100, 167**

**Fiscal year ends, 114**

**Folio Views, 126–128, 151**

*Foreign Currency Translation* **(FAS 52), 58, 86–87**

*Foreign Currency Translation* **(FAS 60), 24**

**Foreign tax credits, 113**

*The Fourth Standard of Reporting* **(AU 500), 100–101, 167–168**

**Franchise revenue, 53**

**Fraudulent tax returns, 117**

**FTB (FASB Technical Bulletins), 20**

**G**

**GAAP:**

hierarchy of, 20–21, 129–130

related-party transactions, 114

**GAAS. *See* Generally Accepted Auditing Standards**

**Gains, taxes on, 116**

**GASB (Governmental Accounting Standards Board), 19**

**Generally Accepted Auditing Standards (GAAS), 93, 94**

**General standards, 18, 23**

*The General Standards* **(AU 200), 98, 166**

**Gift taxes, 117**

**Glossary (in Current Text), 24**

**J**

Job training, 83
John Wiley & Sons, Inc., 3, 4
Journal entries, 158
Jump links, 17

**K**

Keyword searches, 2–3
  correct spelling for, 83
  of CTs, 23
  in FARS, 19
  with FARS CD, 11
  older and newer terminology in, 32
  of OPs, 22
  search within feature, 19
  for tax issues, 114

**L**

Leases, 57, 75–77
  *Accounting for Leases* (FAS 13), 52
  *Amendments to Existing
    Pronouncements to Reflect
    Rescission of Statements 4, 44, and
    64* (FAS 145), 77
  capital, 75
  operating, 75
  standards relating to, 52
Legal Information Institute of
  Cornell University Law School, 7–8,
  12
Liabilities, 79–80
  *Accounting for Transfers and
    Servicing of Financial Assets and
    Extinguishment of Liabilities* (FAS
    140), 88–89
  *The Fair Value Option for Financial
    Assets and Financial Liabilities*
    (FAS 159), 66, 83–84
  tax, 113
Life insurance, 83
Linkages among standards, 75–85
  business combinations, 84–85
  employee benefits, 82–83
  investments, 83–84
  leases, 75–77
  liabilities, 79–80
  not-for-profits, 85
  revenue recognition, 77–78

stockholders' equity, 80–82
Loan impairment, 79
Long-lived assets, 41, 89
Losses:
  capital, 116
  net, 32, 80

**M**

Marketable securities, 58
Medical expense deductions, 113
Minority interest, reporting, 67

**N**

Net income, 32, 80
Net loss, 32, 80
New standards, test questions on,
  67–68
NextPage, Inc., 126, 127
NFPs (not-for-profits), 85
*Noncontrolling Interests in
  Consolidated Financial
  Statements—an Amendment of ARB
  51 Combinations* (FAS 160), 67, 84
Nonmonetary transactions:
  *Accounting for Nonmonetary
    Transactions* (APB 29), 36, 41
  *Exchanges of Nonmonetary Assets*
    (FAS 153), 36, 64
Nonpublic traded entities, standards
  for, 93, 94
Nonreciprocal transfer with owners,
  81
Not-for-profits (NFPs), 85
Notice to Schedule (NTS), 6, 7, 9
Numbers, entering, 157

**O**

*Omnibus Act* (APB 10), 38
*Omnibus Act* (APB 12), 38
OPEB. *See* Other postretirement
  benefits
Operating leases, 75
Operations:
  *Reporting the Results of Operations*
    (APB 9), 38
  *Reporting the Results of Operations:
    Discontinued Events and
    Extraordinary Items* (APB 30), 41–
    42